Mom, Dad
Are You
Listening?

What People are saying about Sonny and his work....

"It's always great to visit with people who have spent time with Sonny Elliott. Their energy and enthusiasm is infectious, their willingness to rise to challenges is inspiring, and their openness to engaging new opportunities enthralling. The real value of Sonny's work is expressed by his clients and deserves high praise."

–R.B. "Bob" Young, Jr.
Former President, Lockheed—EMSCO

"The vast majority of people I have seen whom Sonny Elliott has coached stand out in their enthusiasm for accomplishment and their willingness to learn. He is magic. Whatever he does helps individuals discover greater access to their capabilities and motivation for excellence. This kind of ability is rare and cannot be found in the words spoken, nor even in the concepts he teaches in themselves. He is a great communicator."

–Tim Gallwey
Author of the best seller *The Inner Game of Tennis*

"Sonny Elliott is one of the most skilled communicators we have come across in some time. If you can only listen to two speakers this next year, listen to Sonny—twice!"

–Howard Stevens, Psychologist
President of the H.R. Chally Group

"I have seen Sonny's family, friends, and clients all grow out of his ability to communicate, and the results of his work are very powerful!"

–Dr. Wayne W. Dyer
Author of the best seller
Your Erroneous Zones

"I told Sonny fifteen years ago he had a book inside him. Now he has written it, and it will make a huge difference to all who desire to enhance family relationships. Which include us all!"

–Dr. Elizabeth Harper Neeld
Author of the best seller *Seven Choices*

"While working with Sonny, I have been enabled in my practice to live my credo: 'to help some, to cure others, to give to all.'"
–Dr. Jane Reldan, M.D.
Telluride, CO

"I have seen Sonny Elliott lead a family through the *Family Connection* process, and was impressed by the empowerment it offers the children."
–Dr. Linda Peterson
Top-selling author of *Children in Distress*

"This information works in the classroom with my students because it's authentic communication."
–Susan Roncone
Teacher, Vista, CA.

"Sonny's *Family Connection* process is the best communication system I've seen, because it puts the power and ownership into the hands of the child or adult who's using it."
–Kimberly White
Teacher, San Francisco, CA.

"With the *Family Connection* process, I now have a way of evaluating my effectiveness as a parent and I get the feedback on what's going on in my child's life."
–Sherri Glover
Mother, Homemaker, Houston, TX.

"What more important thing can we give our world, ourselves, than stronger, healthier families? Seize this opportunity to strengthen yours."
– W Mitchell, Top-selling author of
It's Not What Happens To You, But What You Do About It

"Sonny writes like he talks – straightforward and truthfully. You quickly learn that you're hearing from a man who walks his talk, and vice versa. You immediately know that you will learn something from him…Something that will benefit you for the rest of your life."
– Warren H. Chaney, Ph.D.
Hollywood, CA

"Teaching children a process like this at this age will be fantastic for them when they are adults."
–Joan Cunnignham,
Montessori teacher, Houston, Texas

Mom, Dad Are You Listening?

By Sonny Elliott

Enhance Family Communications and Relationships While Teaching Your Children Leadership Skills

SKYSTONE
PUBLISHING
P.O. Box 18731
Reno, Nevada 89511

Mom, Dad, Are You Listening?

Enhance Family Communications and
Relationships While Teaching Your
Children Leadership Skills

 PUBLISHING
P.O. Box 18731, Reno, Nevada 89511
e-mail: sonny@sonnyelliott.com

Copyright © 2000, Sonny Elliott

Library of Congress Card Number: 99-94945
ISBN: 0-9648895-5-2

To order, and for shipping information, please contact **BOOKMASTERS** at:

http://www.bookmaster.com

or

800-247-6553

or

BOOKMASTERS, INC.

P.O. Box 388, Ashland, OH 44805

or fax: 419-281-6883

10   9   8   7   6   5   4   3   2   1

Published in association with Conscious Books
Reno, Nevada 1-800-322-9943.

Cover by Robert Howard Graphic Design
Fort Collins, Colorado

Author photograph: Sue Elliott

Book design by Paul Cirac, White Sage Studios
Drawer G, Virginia City, Nevada

Printed and bound in The United States of America

Table of Contents

Note

*In this age of politically correct phrasing,
terms like "Blacks" and "Indians" are
considered insulting and demeaning. I have
used these terms in the text of my autobiography,
only to illustrate the culture of the time. I
grew up in a highly prejudiced society, and
for the sake of understanding, I have retained the
words that were used commonly during that time.
No insult or derogation of any
ethnic group is intended or implied.*

*This book is dedicated to my family: my
mother, Erna Kloster; my brothers Paul and
Terry; Georgia Kyle, the mother of our sons
Duane and Randy; my second partner,
Patty Elliott; my Soul Mate, Sue, and our four
precious boys with whom we were
privileged to spend part of our journey
as they grew into fine young men:
Duane, Randy, Jerran, and Andy.*
Thank you.

Acknowledgments

There are many people to acknowledge for their contributions to this book. I am optimistic that my writing reflects how profoundly I appreciate all they have collectively contributed to the quality of my family, my life, and my work.

Dr. Elizabeth Neeld was the first person who, in the early eighties, said to me, "Sonny, you have a book inside you," and it was Dr. Warren Chaney who said, "Sonny, write it now!"

I have had the privilege, of working with many author/lecturers who have made a huge difference in the quality of my life: Werner Erhard, R.B. (Bob) Young, Jr., Tim Gallwey, Dr. Wayne W. Dyer, Sandy Vilas, Tom Crum, Rhea Zackich, W Mitchell, Dr. Gene Dongieux, Anthony Robbins, Dr. Gary McLeod, Robert Schulhof, and Dr. Dean Bellavia. Without their insight, influence and coaching, my journey through life would not have been nearly as fulfilling. I thank each of them for their contributions.

I also want to thank my independent editor, Jeanne Rowden, for her continuous support in crafting this work, as well as the guidance from Dan Poynter. And, what can I say about Dr. Linda Peterson, and Dr. Leon Leonard who greeted my "finished" manuscript with a zeal for editing that sent me back to the beginning when I thought I was finished! To them and to my "Family Connection" Partners, Thank you!

And last, but not least, I would like to thank my co-conspirator in the trenches, Joan Garbo.

Foreword

What works these days? Almost nothing! Now, that's an unfortunate statement – but too often, too true. How many of us have picked up book after book on behavioral awareness and self improvement at the local bookstore? Worse yet, we probably bought the book and took it home with us. In our hearts lurked an intense desire to improve our communications, develop a deeper more intimate relationship with our significant other, understand our children a bit better…and yes, dare we hope – to even improve ourselves in the process.

So what happened? We got home and somewhere between the bathroom and the easy chair we examined our purchase. Yep, there it was - the same tired old formulas for self development. Endless chapters were spent explaining why men were from one planet and women were from another. It's as if we weren't smart enough to have figured that one out on our own.

As we read on, the "new" book provided infinite detail on why we were "OK" along with everybody else in the world. Now, I have to admit - that one puzzled me. I knew I was "OK" but I wondered about everyone else. I particularly questioned the ones I lived with. My wife could be cranky and that wasn't "OK." I had five kids – three teenagers at a time – and "OK" is never a term to describe a teenager. They belonged in the same self improvement book as with Mars and Venus. After all, we all know that teenagers are aliens who just happen to reside where we do – at least until they get their first car. No, somehow this line of reasoning fell short of clear thinking.

What I could never get over in all those books was the unending list of terms…the "lingo." You know, the special buzz words you learned so you could spring them on an unsuspecting other when they failed to perform the way the "new" book dictated.

Oh yeah - you really enhanced the intimacy with your spouse or co-worker when you told them about their problems. Nothing increases understanding like laying out another's shortcomings. Remember their response the first time you tried out your book's new vocabulary: "I see my dear that you're persisting in exhibiting the parent side of your personality which no doubt is the result of a right brain challenge in your cortex! Obviously, you neglect to comprehend the potential emotional impact of my dialoging with you. Unfortunately, you've never learned, as I have in my book, *Excellent Communication And Instant Love With Everyone,* that persistence meets resistance. And, now that I have discerned your 'game' behavior, it's all over. Oh yes, by the way – thanks for sharing!"

Yep, I'll bet it didn't take many of those discussions before you realized that most of what is written about human behavior wasn't written for humans…perhaps not even by humans. Well - that's about to change. The book you're holding is different, much different. It works. What a "novel approach" you're probably saying. I thought so too.

I'm a film director where very little is real. My whole life is taken up with non-reality. I spend most of my waking hours talking with people, many of whom aren't real, either. To cope, I've developed my own personal "game" behavior. I've convinced people that there's a lot to "directing" when really – you only have to memorize two words – action and cut. Say those words right and people will think you're a genius. Which brings me to my point. Sonny Elliott, the author of this book, is one. A genius, I mean…not a point…although he makes some very good ones.

I've directed Sonny in many successful television productions. I've heard him speak to exceptionally large groups of people and I've had the good fortune to know him on a very personal level. To be candid - I'm impressed. I was impressed when I filmed his very first infomercial *(he's done over four).* Unlike most infomercials, his testimonials weren't faked. In fact they were just the opposite. I couldn't get people to stop talking about what a great guy he was. They went on and on. Many spoke of how Sonny's work had saved their marriages, their children, and yes - even their lives. Just as impressive, his testimonials flew to our film location from all over the nation…and all, on their own ticket. I'd never seen that.

Hey, come on now! People *that* committed are saying something about what you're getting ready to read, aren't they? Of course they are! When thousands upon thousands of everyday people use Sonny's techniques and swear by them – well – you just know, the boy has got to be doing something right. And, he is. He understands the human psyche as few others do. Better yet, Sonny relates what he knows in a practical way that one can easily understand and immediately use. There's no fancy list of psychological terms here to learn. There's no endless description of game behaviors or for that matter, there's no discussion of Mars, Venus, or other weird stuff.

Sonny writes like he talks – straightforward and truthfully. You quickly learn that you're hearing from a man who walks his talk and vice versa. You immediately know that you will learn something from him…something that will benefit you for the rest of your life.

You've made a good choice to buy this book. Makes you feel good doesn't it?

Happy reading or even better – as a result of Sonny's book, "happy living"!!!

Warren H. Chaney, Ph.D.
Hollywood, CA
February, 1999

Introduction

I was sitting in my chair, looking off into space, wrapped up in my own thoughts, when I heard my wife, Sue, calling my name. "Sonny," she said, "Sonny. Where did you go? What was the call about?" I had, just a few minutes earlier, hung up the phone. I came out of the office, refocused, and came back to the present moment. "It was Herb," I told her, "His mother died."

Herb and his family were our good friends. Sue and I were both saddened by their loss. But it was not his mother's death that prompted Herb's call. He'd brought his mother to live with his family several months earlier, knowing that she was ill, and would not have much longer to live. Herb, his wife, and four children gave his mother a lot of nurturing and love during those last months. It was not her demise that was so surprising; it was the action and reaction of his youngest child, eight year old Hunter.

In the last hours of his mother's life, Herb and his family gathered around their beloved mother and grandmother. After she passed, the family went downstairs to the living room where they all grieved. Somewhere in the midst of the bereavement, Hunter spoke up and got everyone's attention. He called a family meeting. He said, "I think that what we need to do is to go back upstairs and say goodbye to Grandma, so that we can all be at peace." The family looked at each other, realizing Hunter's incredible insight. The family went back upstairs, gathered around the bed, and each, in their own personal way, said "goodbye" to Grandma. Each member of the family spoke, and each member of the family shared with the others what was in their heart.

The foundation for the family meeting was a process I had brought to the family several years earlier. At that time, Hunter was only four years old. While the meeting was going well with the older children and the parents, Hunter tended to wander in and out of the meeting at will. Sometimes he would laugh; sometimes he would get us laughing. Occasionally he would appear to be listening; other times he would ignore us. Sometimes his comments were appropriate, but often they made no connection to the topic at all. Through it all, I noticed that he did appear to have an interest in the family meeting. He kept coming back and he did interject, despite the fact that he was so young.

In the intervening years, Hunter grew, and he became more involved with the family meetings that were held from time to time. When his grandmother died, he took the lead and conducted the family meeting. He showed his involvement and shed light on what those family meetings had meant to him. At the moment of his grandmother's death, Hunter was the only one in the family to see the possibilities clearly.

When Hunter's father related this story to me, he said that this was one of the most moving interactions he had ever witnessed. Not only did he call to tell me about Hunter, he also called to thank me again for teaching his family *The Family Connection* process, a process that is especially powerful in times of sorrow. As I listened to Herb on the phone, I realized that I wanted to share this process with others; and I have. I have worked in schools, on TV, and in families' homes. The book you are holding in your hand is the result of a journey started long ago. I reflect on this earlier time, a time that changed my life and brought me direction.

It was Houston in the mid-seventies. Texas was riding high on the wave of oil and power. The Dallas Cowboys were America's Team, their cheerleaders were some of the most well known women in the world, and a prime time Texas-style soap opera was the most popular show on TV. I'd come to Houston to make my fortune, to become a Player, to have it all.

But one morning, I woke up in a one-room apartment, by myself. I was in the middle of a second divorce. My two teenage sons, living with their mother, were not speaking to me. In the background that morning, I heard a Peggy Lee song. Over and over again, I heard, "Is that all there is?" I was vulnerable that morning as I got into my old car and headed for a job for which I had no passion. And on the way, I pulled over to the side of the road and started crying. The gentle tears soon turned into gut-wrenching sobs. It seemed to me that life really wasn't worth living, yet in that moment, I knew I had no alternative. I became aware that I had to learn to communicate. I had to learn to tell the truth, first to myself, then to others.

That morning, my life took a new direction, a direction in which I am still moving today. Out of that fragmented moment, I found myself becoming what I am today: an ongoing student of communication. I have been with thousands of people, including couples, families, and business groups over the past twenty years, teaching, sharing, and presenting my work on communication and relationship skills.

I want to share with you what I've learned. With the tools you will find in this book, you, like I, can change the direction of your life. You can be in harmony with your children, your spouse, your family, your friends, and even your coworkers. You can grow together in love, understanding, and appreciation. It's all through a process I call *The Family Connection.*

–Sonny Elliott
Reno, Nevada, July, 1999

CHAPTER 1

Life Is Relationships

My grandmother was a pioneer. In her lifetime, she was witness to the westward migration, the invention of the car, man's first flight, radio, and then television. She lived in a period when the world took off and humankind made incredible advances.

I asked her about the world; what was the thing that she thought was the biggest event. She would just shake her head and say, "I don't remember. My memory isn't what it used to be." One day, however, as we sat and chatted, my grandmother smiled and got a faraway look in her eye. She told me of a time when she was a young girl. She lived on a farm that was a stopping place for the wagon trains moving west. The migration was almost over, and what turned out to be the last wagon train had stopped at her family's farm to rest and stock provisions. They stayed several days. In that wagon train was a little girl, the same age as my grandma. The two girls took an instant liking to each other and became fast friends.

Grandma's older brother had more than once warned her about Brownie, a horse on the farm that was wild and unpredictable. He'd often told her to stay away from the questionable creature. But Grandma and her new friend, Lorrie, ignored him and rode that horse for the next three days – all over the farm and down to the glens and creeks. Time came one day that Lorrie had to go. Grandma's eyes became misty as she turned to me and said, "I often wonder what became of Lorrie. I never saw her again."

My grandmother, who had lived to see man go from horse and buggy to the Space Age, did not remember the accomplishments of history. Her memories were of relationships.

For the past two decades, I have spoken with tens of thousands of people of all ages and walks of life. The young speak of goals, of ideas and accomplishments. The old speak of relationships, of family. Invariably, they wish they had spent more time with their children. They wished they had spent more quiet time together, more intimate time. It is always about relationships, they would tell us with a melancholy tear in the eye, as they related that 'relationship' is where the joy in life lay. Their regrets are that they had not participated more fully in the relationships of life. I have yet to meet a person who, at the end of life says, "I wish I had worked more hours or I wish I had made more money." The elderly speak of relationships. For years and years, my family and I would go to old age homes and talk with people who had no visitors. Sometimes we would take little gifts that were always welcome. It was fun for those we visited and those moments reminded us of life's true purpose: sharing our hearts, being in relationships, about who we are, and why we are here. It's about relationships. It's not about anything else, though our society is so often focused on everything *but* relationships. When we visited with these elderly people, I would ask the same question almost every time: "If you had your life to live over again, what would you do differently? What would you do over again, if anything?" I was naïve in the beginning. I thought people would talk about traveling more, or making more money, or retiring in a better home. I thought the answers would be focused on materialistic things. Initially, I was very surprised, but over time learned to expect something different. No, they don't wish for *things*. They wish for relationship.

Life *is* relationships. Granted, ideas and accomplishments play a major role in our lives, in our self-esteem, but the ideas and accomplishments mean nothing if we have no one to share them with. Without relationships, life's accomplishments often feel empty.

Looking back on my experiences at the rest homes and the insight that my grandmother left with me, I've realized that to just go out and spend your life gathering stuff and more stuff is a limiting reason to live. Simply put, the bottom line in life is relationships. It's about our children. It's about our brothers and sisters. It's about Mama and Daddy and our grandparents. Accumulation of wealth is a fun game to play, but not the most meaningful; it's just one way to participate while we are here on this planet. The bigger purpose is to discover who we are, to discover what is in our hearts. The only way to enhance that discovery process is through relationships. I'm sure you and I both know people who have amassed great wealth, yet they are unhappy with their lives. We also know people who don't even know how to spell the word, "wealth," yet they are incredibly happy with their lives. The differ-ence, as far as I can see, always comes down to the quality of relationships that these people have. Our well being, our health, our future happiness correlates directly to the amount of time and energy and love that we have for our fellow human beings, starting with those who are near and dear to us.

You know this. You know that relationships are the most impor-tant thing in our lives. Otherwise you would not be reading this book. You *want* to have meaningful relationships. You *want* to be in harmony with those you

Relationships are the essence of life!

love. You *want* to make life more meaningful, more enriching. Yet, you wonder why life is so stressful, why everything just seems to get piled higher and higher. Perhaps it seems the only time you and your spouse talk is after the kids go to bed; and by then, you are both too tired to put much energy into the conversation.

Researcher, Dr. Richard Peletier, in a study published several years ago, indicated that only seven percent of our population, at any one time expe-riences being wealthy, healthy, and happy at the same time (wealth being subject to one's interpretation). In other words, ninety-three percent of all the people in America die lonely, broke, or ill. This would suggest that the foundation of relationships is the missing ingredient.

Perhaps this sounds familiar: you remember when your teen daughter was a child; how much simpler it all seemed. Now she is seems surly, silent, manipulative, and whiny. The two of you never seem to have fun anymore, and every time you speak with her, it's to reprimand, nag, or blame.

Or you and your nine year-old have just had yet another argument or upset about cleaning his room. He thinks you're mean and can't understand why his room has to be clean if you leave your junk all over the house.

You all love each other, and you want to feel the closeness, the intimacy, more often than just on Christmas morning. You want it every day. You have a good relationship with your family, with those you love, but there seems to be so much antagonism. It is said that we give the best of ourselves to those we know the least, and the worst of ourselves to those we love the most. How true...

My intention with this book is to help you see what it is that blocks intimacy, to recognize what it is you and your loved ones want to achieve, and how to go about achieving it. I want you to have harmony. I want you to have fulfilling relationships. I want you to bring your love and caring for each other to new levels. It is what I would have wanted for my own inner child, who, because he never got it, feels compassionate for other children.

CHAPTER 2

Early Life

My mother, like my grandmother, had the pioneer spirit. She was born in Dodge City, Kansas in 1924. My father was a soldier and was stationed on an aircraft carrier during World War II. My mother, pregnant with me, ventured to California. She moved in with her aunt and went to work for the war effort as one of those gallant women so fondly referred to as "Rosie the Riveter." She worked long hours and did not have the luxury of time nor the energy to care for a small infant, so I was left in the care of an aunt; I later learned this aunt did not care much for me. During that time, my father died, killed by what is known as 'friendly fire.' This tragic error of the war left my mother without a husband, and me without a father. He died not ever knowing that I was even conceived.

My first three years were spent in California. My mother remarried when I was three years old. As part of the marriage promise, the man my mother married adopted me and changed my name. What my mother didn't know when she married him was that Vic was an alcoholic and an abuser. His weapons were both physical and emotional. He had promised to take care of me, when in fact, he did everything but that.

Psychologists tell us that by the age of three, our self-esteem (or lack of) is pretty well in place. What self-esteem means here is how one relates to one's environment; not the material goods, but the human relationships. Researchers also show that during the first year of life, an individual can determine how safe it will be to give love or to be loved. This research indicates that the level of trust we have for others is determined by the end of the first year of life. When we cry, are we held? Are we nurtured? Are we surrounded by loud noise and anger, or is it a safe environment? With my mother working all the time, I was left in the care of an aunt who did not love me, who did not give consistent and loving care. As a result, by age three, I had already unknowingly determined that I could not trust others and that I was not worthy of love, all the result of a weak foundation of self-esteem.

HARVEST

When I was five years old, my stepfather, fresh out of the service, moved my mother and me from California back to Dodge City. My grandparents farmed a section of land some twenty miles from Dodge. We visited their farm on occasion and I have happy memories of those times.

I was a small boy playing in the yard one day when I teased a turkey who wandered around the barnyard. The turkey was much larger than I and had a distinct advantage over a small and frightened child. He attacked me and pinned me to the ground where he pecked and scratched and tore at me. My grandmother came to the rescue, shooed the turkey away, and took me to the house for first aid and hugs. That night we had turkey for dinner – and I was the guest of honor. I will never forget how my grandmother saved me from a fate worse than death. On top of that, I got to be the hero, the center of attention. In my eyes, my grandmother was the hero, and I felt safe and secure when I was with her. Little did I know that a belief was formed that day, and would come back to me in the future, and shows how *everything* that happens to us is connected.

I especially loved the farm at wheat harvest time. When it came time to harvest the wheat, my grandfather would hire a lot of farmhands to help. This was an exciting time, full of new faces, long days and the sights, smells, and sounds of the farm. Machinery was always breaking down, but it didn't stop the workers. They would work by hand while repairs were being made. I especially loved riding the combine, watching while it crawled through the fields, cutting the stalks and separating the wheat from the chaff. When the combine was full, the wheat would be dumped into waiting trucks that would take it to the silos on the farm or drive it into town to the huge grain silos. During the harvest that combine would just keep going, seemingly day and night.

Everyone worked from long before sunup until long after sundown. To save time, lunch was served in the field. Not until all the day's harvest was stored and the equipment cleaned up and put away did the field hands come to supper. It was at this time, around a gigantic table, that they discussed the day's events; what worked, what didn't work, what could make the process easier and better.

The rule for children was to be seen and not heard. But if we were quiet and attentive, we would be allowed to join the grownups and listen in. It was around this table that I first heard conversations about working together, about teamwork. Harvest was a time when people of many backgrounds, nationalities, and personalities came together. These were men who had very different beliefs about everything: from the food they ate, to the types of women they would marry to the way children should behave, even to the way wheat should be harvested. Many of these workers had immigrated to the Sunbelt states. This was America's breadbasket and it became home to farmers from all over the world. In the eyes of a five year-old, it was the most magical and wonderful place to be. Looking back, I realize that around Grandma's table, I had actually experienced my first family meetings. It took me thirty-five years to come back around and actually design a process that would accommodate meetings that, at one time in our history, naturally took place pretty much everywhere in the country.

As I look through an adult's eyes to that time, I now see a set of values there. I see that there was incredible harmony. I see that men were more focused on the result, rather than on whose fault it was when something didn't work out. They had the big picture, the bottom line in mind. These men and women were so focused that they did not major in minor things. Today I see just the opposite. The family is not in touch with the big picture – harmony and peace. The family is more interested in who did what and whose fault it is. This frequently leads to blame, shame and guilt.

The process I have designed over the years, if followed properly, negates blame, shame, guilt, and finger pointing. It actually helps families concentrate on a bigger purpose, a family that is committed to being in relationship.

Those wonderful days on the farm come to mind infrequently; usually there is something that triggers the memory. Have you ever heard a song that reminded you of your prom date, an odor that reminds you of someplace long ago and far away? Sometimes when I pull into an old service station, (there are still a few left in the smaller towns) almost always, as I get out of my car and am assailed by the aroma of gas and grease, I am transported back in time to when I was five years old, and it was time for the harvest. I can *be* in that moment, smell the odors, see my grandfather driving the combine. I can see the wheat fields being cut; I can see the truck drivers hauling the wheat to the silos. Future courses of action are determined for the most part by those remnants of the past.

I always wanted to stay on my grandparents' farm. However, we always returned to our home on the outskirts of Dodge City. We were very poor. We lived next to the dog pound. You can imagine the noise I lived with day and night. I walked to school in all kinds of weather. I would love to say I walked barefoot twenty miles both ways, but in truth, it was maybe three-quarters of a mile at most.

SCHOOL

I can never forget my first day in school. Although I didn't realize it at the time, that first day of school took a large toll on me in later years. By the end of that first day, I'd learned many things: that I was one of the poorest children in the class, that I wasn't as smart as other children, and that somehow all the other children in the class knew it too. Over time, I noticed that the children from nicer homes – the ones with nice clothing – somehow ended up in the front of the classroom. They spoke up more in class; they were listened to more often. Children such as I tended to grav-itate to the back of the class, where we kept to ourselves and looked down to avoid eye contact with the teacher. We were also dressed very poorly. I saw the difference, and by the end of that first day, I'd made decisions that directed my thoughts and actions for more than thirty years, even though I was only seven years old and all I did that day was sit in class, being still, being by myself.

Psychologists tell us that by the time a child is seven to nine years old, they have learned more than they will learn in the entire rest of their lives. A child by this age has learned about trust and mistrust. They have learned how to reason, and the foundation of self-esteem is firmly in place. This innate knowledge is the cornerstone that directly affects the child for the rest of his or her life.

During the second grade, I became accustomed to being picked on. I think it was because I was a quiet student, and poorly dressed. I certainly showed up as an ignorant and non-participatory student. One day, three white boys told me they were going to get me after school. I was petrified. One of my biggest fears was getting beaten, and I knew what three boys could do to another boy. I was terrified. When class let out, I tried to sneak away and not be seen. Of course, that didn't work. As the three boys circled me, a crowd gathered to watch and to cheer the boys on. I had no friends, no alliances, and no allegiances. As the boys were taunting me and working up the courage to attack, a black boy came out of nowhere. I didn't know him, had never seen him before. He stood taller than all of us; I suspect he must have been in a higher grade. He stepped in beside me, looked at the three boys and said, "You'll have to fight me first. You're not going to touch this boy." He warned them that he'd better not hear of them bothering me again. Sure enough, the boys walked away and the crowd dispersed. I stood there, shocked, relieved, scared, and confused. When I tried to thank the boy, he just laughed and said, "Aw, those guys won't mess with you again." Indeed, they did not. I don't recall ever seeing my rescuer again. I always wondered what it was that made him show up that day at that time. I remember too, wishing he had been a little bigger so I could have taken him home to protect me from Vic.

Vic, being an alcoholic, lost jobs regularly. We found ourselves moving from small town to small town throughout Kansas, Nebraska, and Missouri. As you can imagine, I soon became lost in the school system. I was always behind. I never caught up, much less got ahead. Moving from town to town, and from school to school, I never got the opportunity to make friends. It seemed to me that I was always the most shabbily dressed kid, and I also seemed to be the one who was picked on the most. I will never forget another incident that happened when I was in the second grade. I was enrolled in yet another new school the third time that year. On that first day, I summoned up the nerve to ask a question. I raised my hand. The teacher called on me. I don't remember the question, but I sure remember the answer. The teacher rolled her eyes, looked around the class, and said, "*Everybody* knows the answer to that, don't we children?" I will never forget the outburst of laughter from the other children, nor will I ever forget the humiliation I felt. Unwittingly, in that horrible moment, I made a decision about myself. I decided I was stupid. Everyone else knew something that I didn't. Somewhere deep inside, I made the decision to never again ask another question in public. I would never show my stupidity again. After that day, I rarely went outside for recess, for it was on the playground that I was teased mercilessly. Instead, I turned to what is still today one of my greatest joys: reading.

I would come to school, barely on time for class. If I did arrive early, I would hide out and read. I stayed in during recess. We could not afford to buy lunch at school. I didn't mind, because then I could stay in the classroom and read while I ate the meals my mother prepared for me. I became a recluse. It was a matter of survival and self-protection. I was different and had to stay separate. It was my way of coping with the frequent moves, the constant shuffling from school to school and town to town.

LIFE AT HOME

Throughout my entire childhood, I was emotionally and physically abused, as was my mother. The five children from her union with Vic that eventually came along were never abused in that way. Somehow, it was different for them. I was the scapegoat. I rarely felt close to my siblings. Oh, there were some fun times with them, but not many. Not only was I not Vic's child, but also, I'm sure that there were times it appeared my mother favored me, given that I was her first, her eldest. She cared for me before she met Vic and after they were married, she certainly went out of her way to protect me from the physical and emotional abuse. Perhaps he needed to punish my mother and me for that. Perhaps he could not accept and resolve that lack of blood tie. Whatever the reasons, I knew that when he came home drunk – which was quite frequently – I had to stay out of his way; I had to hide. Often it didn't work. His normal procedure was to take off his belt, fold it in two, and make me bend over something. Then he would beat me on my back and on my buttocks. Even though I was brutalized, he rarely left physical marks. Of course, there were scars all over my emotions, but at that age, I was not aware of the difference between emotional pain and physical pain. On one occasion, in violent anger, he grabbed a chain and hit me with it. Another time he used a large piece of wood as a club. One incident stays fresh in my mind. It was a cold, snowy night. Vic sent me out into the dark. Wind blew sharp needles of frozen snow, stinging my eyes. I can remember crying, the tears almost freezing on my face. I can still hear my howls of anguish, which began in anticipation of the beating. When I came back with a small stick, he slapped me and sent me back out into the snow to get a much larger one or, he said, I would really pay. My mother would try to intercede, but that only resulted in a beating for her, too.

Such was my early life: I was raised by a devout mother who was, herself, brutalized and who was unable to help me, since she, too lived in fear of her husband. I was a stepchild, deathly afraid of my stepfather. I have no memory of playing with him. I don't remember getting much help with my homework. All I remember is that I lived each day just trying to survive, to avoid the blows, to hide away. All I ever wanted was to grow up as fast as I could so I could leave home and be free.

Looking back on those early years of my life, I can readily see that if we'd had any kind of communication process, any kind of format or formula to actually sit down and talk, I honestly believe that the horror of my childhood would not have happened. In that day and time there was no format. Children were to be seen and not heard, and if a child did speak up, it was thought to be sassing or back talk rather than making an inquiry. Even having said that, in my heart I would like to think that some kind of process like the one in this book would have made life look much different for all of us.

THE JOCKS

In my travels from school to school, I observed the other children, the teachers, and the interactions of whatever community I had been dragged into. I found one thing that was always consistent. At each school, there was a group of boys who seemed to get away with more. These boys were cutups in class, they ruled the playground, and they got special privileges that the rest of us did not. These were the athletic boys – the jocks. They got recognition in sports and it poured over into other aspects of their lives. They were more popular. Girls buzzed around them like honeybees. It seemed that their grades were better.

By the time I was in the third grade, I decided that I, too would get on a baseball team. Then I would be popular and get to cut up. I thought if I became an athlete, I would be validated and somehow overcome the shabby clothes, the poor grades my poor verbal abilities. I thought if I could only make a team, I would overcome what I learned later was a total lack of self-esteem. I now see that was my way of attempting to hide my feelings of insecurity, inferiority, and my need for everyone's approval.

Here I was, nine years old, with a dream. I never got an allowance, and in actuality, there wasn't a great deal of work that was suited for a nine year-old boy. But my mother found me a job with a widow woman, pulling weeds in her flowerbeds. Mom would take me in the old Chevy to the woman's house. I would work a couple of hours until about dark, and the widow would pay me fifty cents. It took several weeks to earn enough money to buy a ball glove.

It wasn't too long before I had saved up three dollars. My mother and Vic took me to a store to buy a baseball glove. I knew as soon as I had the glove that I would be picked to be on the team and then I could be a hero. Vic picked out a glove; I paid for it and took it home proudly.

Now remember, I had no knowledge of baseball, nor did Vic. We had never played together, we did not spend time together, we did nothing together. All I knew of baseball was from watching the other children as they played. Nevertheless, I was proud that first day at recess when I put my books away and joined the others on the field. I took to the outfield. It was relatively empty, so I could still be alone. I was incredibly shy and the outfield afforded me a bit of distance.

I will never forget my excitement and fear as that ball came to me the first time. I held my shiny new glove out in front of me and kept my eye on the ball, wishing it into my glove. It did not happen, and I did not catch the ball. However, it had nothing to do with my skill; it was the glove. The ball bounced out of my hand as if I had hit it with the bat myself. I flubbed the play and heard the jeers and ridicule from the other children.

I was humiliated. The glove my stepfather had picked out was nothing more than a toy glove. There was no pocket. It was not the soft, formed glove worn by the other boys. It was better suited for tennis than baseball. As soon as I could, I buried the glove at the bottom of the trash. If anybody asked, I said I had lost it. I never joined in the games at that school again.

The incident did not keep me from trying out for sports, though. Since we moved so often, each new school was a new slate, a place for me to try out for a team, to try to make it into that special group, to be a hero. I tried out with borrowed gloves; I tried and tried. I realized then that it was not the glove that made the difference whether or not I made the team. Yet, no matter how hard I tried, I didn't make the first team. I didn't make the second team and I didn't make the third team. What I didn't realize, ignorant of life as I was, that, to make the team, one had to practice. I didn't know that the boys had fathers at home who would practice with them, who showed them how to throw, how to bat, how to catch. I had never seen this. I had few friends, so I was rarely invited to any-

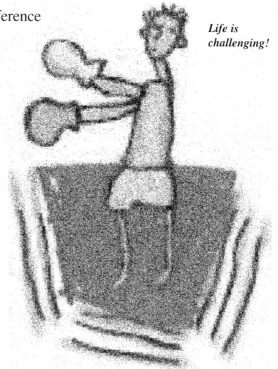

Life is challenging!

one's house. Everywhere we went, we seemed to be on the wrong side of the tracks. We were the kids who were either ridiculed or ignored. So we never learned what other families did, how they lived, how they supported each other. We were the outcasts.

It was probably about this time that I found myself being labeled a loser. I don't know where it started, but I do know that I believed it. You can imagine an eight year-old boy, feeling humiliated, dejected, and rejected by his peers. Getting put down by his teachers. Walking home from school, knowing that most likely he would be beaten again when he got there. At that age, I had not much of anything to look forward to, except growing up and running away. All I knew was pain – or fear of pain – of one sort or another from the time I woke up in the morning until I went to sleep at night.

FINALLY A HERO

There were occasions when I did get on a team. But they were few and far between. They were not memorable, not lasting and they were nothing I could anchor to. I do recall, however, when I was eleven years old and in the sixth grade. We were living in a small lead-mining town, not far from the Missouri border. It was an old place with a run-down house and barn, set on about twenty acres. There was a small creek running through the property, with trees and a ravine. On the other side of the house, there were more trees. It was there that we built our forts and played "Cowboys and Indians." I played mostly with my brothers and sisters, and once in a while other kids would show up to play. So, while I had few friends, once in a while, the routine would change, just because kids would want something different to do.

There were about seven acres of tall grass on the property. This is where I would attempt to practice baseball by myself. I rarely had people to practice with; nevertheless, I set up the bases and got an old bedspring to use as a backstop should we ever get the opportunity to play a game.

It was a hot, dry, boring day. Even the clouds seemed lethargic in the hot summer sun. Soon that all changed. My brothers, sisters and I noticed smoke along the dusty main road. Being made of dirt, the cars and trucks driving it would send up huge clouds of dust. We were accustomed to that sight. What we saw this day was something very different. Today, the breeze kicked up flame from some discarded cigarette or match. We lived about a mile from any other houses, and since we had no phone, the arrival of a fire truck was highly unlikely. But the kids in the nearby houses saw the fire, and soon there were a dozen or more of us, excited and ready to fight the good fight.

We had no running water. Instead, we drew buckets of water from the well. We soaked feed sacks in the water drawn from the well and beat back what in our eyes was a raging inferno. I can still feel the burning in my arms and the blisters that formed on my hands as I lowered the bucket into the well, drew up the next bucketful of water and poured it onto the singed burlap sacks. The clouds seemed to be in a frenzy now, the trees bent, the birds screamed and rodents ran hysterically under our feet, away from the fire. All that came between the fire and our house was a group of children, trying valiantly to extinguish the flames.

Finally, we won. We conquered the flames. We, a rag-tag group of children, had taken on nature and won. We felt triumphant. Our smiles broke through our soot-stained faces as Mama loaded us all into the old Chevy. Sitting on laps, hanging out the windows, we celebrated our victory at the Dairy Queen. Mama was so proud! Even today, I pull out that picture and remember the satisfaction I felt.

Returning to school that fall, we found ourselves to be heroes. In the course of telling the tale, I'm sure the story grew and grew, and we convinced ourselves that we had conquered the fire that surely would have swept across the entire state of Kansas, had we not been there to save the day. For an incredible few days, I knew what it was like *not* to feel like a loser; I knew what it was like *not* to be focused on what was waiting for me at home. For a few days, I got to be a hero. For the second time in my life (the first having been when I survived the turkey attack) I got admiring glances. For a few days, I was someone else. But soon my claim to fame faded, and everyone moved on. But it was a memory I cherished and would return to time and time again. In my heart of hearts, it was a flame that kept burning, a light for those many dark times. And in my child's mind, I knew that there was an alternative to being a loser. I knew, because I had experienced it, however so briefly. And it was based on circumstances, which later in life would prove to have been a costly decision.

BIGOTRY IN THE REAL WORLD

I was in the seventh grade and living in yet another shack on the wrong side of yet another little town. Across from us lived an elderly black couple. I remember being told not to associate with those people, that they were bad; all kinds of negative, derogatory things. Of course, the only memory I had up until then was of a black boy, who, from my point of view, saved my life. I was actually eager to meet these people, but I knew I had to be careful. Many times when Vic was gone, I would go across the road to see the couple. I always went alone. And I always learned a lot from them. They were fine people. They kept a big vegetable garden, which I would help them tend to on occasion. They treated me well. I still love gardening, and learning from this couple is where I got started. They knew we were poor; they knew we went without meals sometimes. After all, I had told them how we sometimes went hungry. I will always remember their generosity. They often sent me home with things from the garden. Mother and I never told Vic. He probably would have killed us for going over there; he hated black people so. But they actually provided a lot of meals for us. Potatoes, corn, peas – we got them all from this wonderful couple. From time to time, they would give us meat when they butchered. My two childhood experiences with blacks were so very contrary to what

I had been told –given the remarks Vic would make – that I became confused. I was too young to question what I had been taught. When we prepared to move, the saddest part was leaving these two people who took me as I was, accepted me, encouraged me and showed me their compassion. They sometimes seemed more like family to me than my own siblings did.

CHAPTER 3

Families

WHAT IS A FAMILY?

What is a family?

The definition of family, as described in the *New Shorter Oxford English Dictionary* six definitions:

> **1.** The servants of a house or establishment; **2.** The staff of a high-ranking military officer or State official; **3.** The descendants of a common ancestor; **4.** A race; a people assumed to be descended from a common stock; **5.** A group of people living as one household; **6.** A group of individuals or nations bound together by political or religious ties;
> **7.** The group of people consisting of one set of parents and their children, whether living together or not; any group of people connected by blood or other relationship.

So we see that "family" is a rather loose term, one that can and does define relationships. In America today, the term family means many things. We have the traditional family: Mom and Dad are married, with children and all are living in the same household. Then we have seven million blended families – single, widowed or divorced parents that come together to create a new family. There are fifteen million single-parent families in the US. Grandparents are raising their grandchildren, without the presence or assistance of the child's parents. Many households consist of two or more families living under one roof.

While all these families are different, with different situations, the bottom line remains the same. All the members of all these families have interactions with each other. They must all work to communicate and get along.

Maggie Scarf, in her book, *Intimate Worlds*, outlines where Americans fall in the functioning of the family dynamic. She states that 6 percent of all families have a severely dysfunctional system, where physical, mental and emotional abuses are the rule. On the other end of the spectrum, another 6 percent have what is considered an ideal relationship – one where each individual is honored and respected and the other members of the family support each member. The remaining balance fall into the middle ground. That leaves 88 percent who have good relationships that could be improved with better communication skills.[1] Let's go back and look where this all started in our culture.

FAMILY OVERVIEW

At the end of World War II, most American families were what we call traditional. The traditional family consists of Mom and Dad, and their children, living together under one roof. The post-war generation was the first to break out of the extended family (grandparents, aunts, uncles, cousins all living in close proximity). Veterans returning from Europe or the Pacific Theater relocated to different states, leaving behind their relatives to settle in a new place. The goal of Americans was just as it had been for generations – the parents work hard to create a life for their children, better than they themselves had. Parents worked to provide a stable home, and save for a college education.

The sixties and seventies were a time of change, of exploration, of throwing out the old. It was at this time that the concept of traditional family was challenged. Communes abounded; it was the era of peace, love, and the rumor that God is Dead. Traditional life, traditional values were challenged and discarded. This led to two decades of selfish behavior. Parents still wanted everything for their children. But the concept of working for it, the concept of patience was replaced by the concept of instant gratification. We no longer had to wait and work for something; we could just put it on a credit card and pay it off later.

Before long, many families were in deep debt. One income no longer paid the bills. The desire for more stuff, more status, led to both parents

working outside the home. That, with the increase in single-parent families, has led to a cycle by which the children have often come to control
the family finances, thus laying the foundation for breakdowns in day-to-
day family operations. Thirty four million children, age twelve and
younger, determine where five hundred *million* dollars in disposable
income goes every year! Children are determining the direction of the
Gross National Product! And, for the first time in America's history, our
children are *not* facing a life that is better than that of the generation
before. This has created many changes in the way we interact with our
children.

CONSEQUENCES VS. PUNISHMENT

We live in a society that today is averse to disciplining its children.
Since the 1950's there has been a trend away from the strict, authoritarian
method of raising children to a permissive, 'do your own thing' style. As
a result, we have a generation of people, many of whom have little or no
regard for authority, boundaries, or self-control. With the headlines full of
children killing children, we are beginning to recognize that, on one hand,
we cannot let our children run wild, and provide no boundaries. But on the
other hand we cannot beat values into them. We damage our children
either way.

Maggie Scarf says that six percent of the families in America today routinely use physical abuse as a form of punishment. Children are being
beaten, kicked, and threatened, all in the name of discipline; or worse yet,
simply as a means of entertainment – abuse for abuse's sake. Physical
abuse is not the only form of torture. There is emotional abuse, and this is
about power and control issues. When we call our children names, when
we laugh at their efforts, when we tear down their self-esteem, we abuse
them just as badly as if we had taken a belt to them. *Some ninety-two percent of children interviewed do not feel safe going to their parents with
their issues!* They fear there will be a penalty, ranging from shame and
blame to corporal punishment. Most adults would never tolerate a cowork-
er or boss telling them that they're stupid, selfish or just plain mean. But
they often dish it out to their children and expect them to take it.

At the other end of the spectrum are the parents who do not discipline
their children at all. Their well-meaning intentions, in many ways can be
just as damaging a form of abuse. Without boundaries or discipline, the

children can grow up to be selfish, uncaring, and unempathetic. Typically, they have no basis for their ethics; morality is a foreign concept. The parents give *things*, they give money, they arrange for lessons and trips for their children, when what the children really want is time with mom and dad. The parents cannot stand to see the children 'do without' and often end up giving far more stuff than the children need. The parents know that they are spoiling the children, but they don't know what to do to change the situation. They don't seem to know how to come to a workable balance.

Parents often – unintentionally, I think – are too permissive with their children in the area of discipline. It's almost like a popularity contest; parents would rather be popular than risk the displeasure of the child. I think some of this stems back to the fact that in most families both parents are working. There is often guilt here. The children are home without the parents, so the parents try to make up for it by being 'buddies' with their children. You know, *it really is okay to say no*. All children push to be in charge. But what they are really doing is looking for boundaries, they're looking for where the line is. Remember, children do what we do; they don't particularly do what we say.

I think one of the main reasons that children misbehave today is because the rules keep changing. The consequences, if any, keep changing. The result of all this is persistent confusion for the child. Parents often change the rules from day to day. The consequences are inconsistent. Often the child is not given a firm sense of right and wrong, of what is appropriate behavior. Frequently, the boundaries are not established or are not clear, especially when the parents keep changing them. The child typically has only one way of figuring this out and that is by pushing back. This lack of consistency is detrimental to the child and can actually hinder his growth and development. Even as he enters adulthood, with all these mixed messages, you can imagine some of the possible turns this young adult might take in life. Ultimately, if the child is not held to account in his home environment, if he does not learn the lessons of honor, integrity, and respect, how can we expect him to go out in life as an adult and be any different?

Several years ago, a Conference Board study of sixth grade children indicated that one of the biggest problems for children is the inability to keep their word about anything, from homework to cleaning their room.

That stems back to the question, what are they learning, or not learning, from their parents? Remember, children are a product of their environment, in almost every way. Often the parents will say x and do y. Parents will say, "Clean your room, or you can't play at Bobby's." The child doesn't clean the room. Something comes up and the parents allow the child to play at

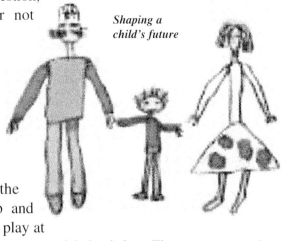

Shaping a child's future

Bobby's. Sometimes it revolves around babysitting. The parent gets the opportunity to do something, so they recant the threat (you cannot go to Bobby's) and allow the child to do what it is that they were earlier told they could not do. This frees the parent to do that non-child activity. Television is another great babysitter. How many parents say, "the TV is off limits until your homework is done?" How many times do those same parents retract the television rule because they just hate it when little Maryann pouts. After all, it gets the parents off the hook.

When a child gets used to parents saying x and doing y, they learn that the parent can't be trusted, that they themselves can get away with things, but most of all, they never learn the art of setting boundaries.

There are endless polls and statistics regarding family life in America. One that especially caught my eye was one that stated that most arguments between couples revolve around the children. Some thirty-two percent of arguments between couples revolve around disciplining the children. Another twenty-five percent of arguments are around decisions having to do with the children, like what to do, where to go, what clothes to buy, what bedtime, what study time, etc. This poll also indicates that of the thirty-two percent who argue about discipline, forty-seven percent revolve around chores, forty percent are around bedtime issues, and twenty-eight percent around schoolwork.

How do we get around these arguments? Be clear on the goal, teach the children discipline. Here are a few guidelines:

1. *Be consistent on the boundaries.* The reason most children break agreements, is because, initially, they are unclear on the agreement, or perhaps the parent keeps changing the agreement. The boundaries must be clear, and the parents must adhere to those boundaries as well. If they should change the boundaries, they need to inform the child before the child breaks the new boundaries that have been put in place. This is especially critical in blended families, where two families have come together with different rules, beliefs, and boundaries. This can be a staging ground for unfavorable behavior. The adults need to agree what the boundaries are, for the blended extended family. One great way to handle this challenging area is for both the parents and children to sit down together, and work out the new rules and boundaries. Then put them in writing to avoid confusion!

2. *Once clear on the boundaries, be consistent with the consequences.* Outline the consequences in advance. One of the great upsets in families is when the parent does not adhere to the boundaries themselves. Follow through is critical. As Tim Gallwey, author of *The Inner Game of Tennis* once told me, "Children have but one job in life, and that is to test their parents." It is the nature of children to push the limits, to see how far they can go, how much they can get away with. Remember, this is supposed to happen! A child will rebel just to see if it can be done. Children are in training to eventually live independently in the world. Again, this means that the parents must be consistent; they cannot back down from the boundaries that have been established. The child needs to see that her parents are secure and confident leaders, not indecisive fence sitters.

3. *See the difference between simple childish behavior and willful defiance of the boundaries.* The term, 'grow up and act your age,' has to be the silliest thing to ever come out of the mouths of adults. You find your five year-old bouncing on the sofa. Your response? "Grow up and act your age!" Think about what you just said. You told a five year-old to act his age. Well that is exactly what he was doing; acting his age. He is not testing you, he is just doing his five year-old thing. Now, had you asked him to pick up his toy cars (a boundary) and he screamed, "No!" and instead, threw them at you, you could safely assume that he is knowingly breaking the rule that should be clear (toys are to be picked up). Take the time before you react to determine the action to take. Take your time; don't react out of anger.

4. *Don't hold the children's violations against him or her.* Once the issue is completed and the child has received the consequences, then drop it. Don't hold their actions against them. Make sure they know you love them, even though you did not approve of their actions. This is an important difference between the person and their behavior. The circumstance is outside of who we really are, outside of our "inner-self." Making mistakes are a valuable means of learning, much more so than success! Make that clarification, then get back into relationship with harmony and affinity.

5. *Above and beyond all, be in relationship with your children.* Love, in the final analysis, is what the child is after. Stephen Covey said it best: "The deepest hunger of the human heart is to be related." Let your love for your children guide your actions. Always ask yourself, how can this conflict be resolved and how can we bring harmony back to the family? Ask yourself *before* you discipline your child. You are sure to find a resolution, and your children will learn from firm boundaries and unconditional love. That is our job as parents and that is the commitment we made when we brought them into the world.

I once observed a father bribe his son to replace some Christmas ornaments he had taken, without permission, off a tree. He said to his son, "Now Billy, if you put those ornaments back on the tree right now, I will take you to the store to buy your own." Initially, it appeared to me that there were no consequences, no paternal control. I actually thought little Billy learned two things: that extortion could get him anything, and there would be no consequences for his actions. But upon further reflection, I realized that this was a six year-old child, and that there *were* consequences; the consequences seemed initially inconsistent from my point of view. The father did exactly what worked in that situation. The child was taught not to steal, to put things back. The child was taught that if the father knew what the child wanted, he could be responsive to the child's wants and decide whether to give the child ornaments or not. In this case the father decided to give the child what he wanted. Had this been a teenage boy, however, this "reward" would not have been appropriate.

Various studies have shown that eighty-eight percent of parents in America think they have a good relationship with their children. But parents spend on average of only five minutes per day in conversation with their children. Three and a half minutes of that are used in instruction and discipline, leaving only one and a half minutes in two-way conversation. How much can you know about a person if you only spend a minute and a half in meaningful conversation? Of course, the average American married couple spends just seven minutes a day in meaningful conversation. Meanwhile, in the same household, the television will be on five to six hours a day.

Once, many years ago, we were on our way to a movie, Sue, Andy, Jerran and I. The boys were in the back seat and they kept poking at each other, raising a ruckus. I'd raise my voice while looking in the mirror, and tell them to stop. They continued the rough housing despite my vocal displeasure. Finally, a light bulb went off. I turned to Sue, winked and whispered, "I've got a solution." When we arrived at the theater, I bought two tickets instead of four. Once inside, I pulled the door attendant aside and told him I was going to park Jerran and Andy right outside the door, and if they even moved, to let me know. Having worked my way through college in a movie theater chain, I had something to build a little bit of a relationship on. The door attendant got the point, and, with a huge grin on his face, agreed to help. The boys were a bit surprised. I turned to them and said, "Movies are a treat for people who don't argue and fight in the car! You are going to sit out here, while your mother and I watch the movie." Andy, always being assertive and willing to move on quickly, said, "Well, then can I have some soda and popcorn?" I nixed that, telling him, "No, popcorn and soda are for the people watching the movie!." There's a water fountain over there." We parked the boys and went in to watch the movie. I did come out many times during the movie to check on the boys, and they did just fine. While it was uncomfortable following through with the consequence, we never had that issue come up again!

The boys finally realized what was happening. There is a distinct difference between consequences and punishment. Punishment is almost always vengeful and hurtful. Consequences are much more powerful. There are consequences if you run a red light, there are consequences if you don't get to work on time, or get to the airport late. Sue and I raised the boys using consequences. If you misbehave in the car, you don't get to see the movie; if you don't do your household chores then you will miss out on your favorite activity. Years later, when the boys were grown, we were all riding somewhere in the car. Jerran and Andy were in the back seat, where they were mildly teasing each other. I looked in the rearview mirror, and with my best angry daddy voice said, "Hey, you guys! Knock it off!" Suddenly we were all back in that memory of when they missed the movie because of their rowdy behavior. This time we all laughed and enjoyed the memory. It may not have been funny to the boys at the time, but as adults, they could look back and remember how they had gotten a lesson in consequences in that theater lobby.

It's been said that laughter is the shortest distance between two people. I've never forgotten that. As the boys sat in the back seat laughing, the saying came to mind and I thought, "how true." Humor, brought to any problem, diminishes the problem instantly. It tends to open up an avenue of possibilities. I've heard it said that it takes seventeen facial muscles to smile and forty-three to frown. It is also said that just thirty seconds of laughter will equal three minutes of good cardiovascular exercise. The point is well taken here. Laughter not only makes the situation much easier to deal with, it's also very healthy for our bodies.

Laughter sheds pain. We often take things far too personally. Easily, we interpret things in the harshest light, taking the low road instead of looking for the bright side. We have robbed children of humor. Remember a time when you said something funny and no one laughed? You felt foolish, so you withdrew. What about the time you said something serious and everyone laughed? Same effect. I think that often, unwittingly, we do the same to our children. But sometimes the consequences are not laughable.

SPANKING

I personally feel that spanking is absolutely inappropriate. When you use spanking as a punishment – and it is punishment, not consequence – it delivers the message that violence solves problems. Often, these children go on to hitting kids at school, and as adults, they end up hitting their spouses. I have a particular aversion to that, having been beaten regularly as a child. I perhaps spanked my young sons twice before realizing it hadn't worked with me; why did I feel that it would work with my boys? I did not want my children to fear me like I had feared Vic. It was much more powerful to use consequences. So often parents justify their anger over a circumstance they disagree with and strike their children. Using communication skills and working out appropriate consequences is much more effective and does not leave emotional and physical scars.

I saw a report in Newsweek[2] that suggested that some seventy- percent of Americans felt that spanking was okay, despite reports from the Academy of Pediatrics saying otherwise. The study indicated that corporal punishment is more accepted in rural areas and among low income families than among college-educated urbanites. Spanking seems to be a cultural belief, an accepted practice among the blue-collar working class, like the one in which I was raised.

A common error made by parents in disciplining their children is that they attempt to discipline when they are angry. Parents rely on their own emotional responses to get the child to cooperate. Unfortunately, this usually results in nothing more than a shouting match; there is no resolution to the conflict. In fact, the child may perceive that the parent has lost control – control of his or her emotions and control of the situation. We as parents represent a justice system to our children. If the parent is on the edge, screaming, crying and flailing about, the child sees that there will be no justice today. Would you respect a boss or co-worker who lost control and cried and screamed at you about it? Of course you wouldn't. You'd think he'd lost his marbles. Your children think the same thing when you scream and cry. By losing your temper, you lose the respect of your children.

One of the more interesting facets of human dynamics occurs around our emotions. Any time an adult is upset, from rolling the eyes in frustration, to outright rage, that adult has just unknowingly, unwittingly reverted back to a childhood emotional state. You literally can look at an upset adult and see what age they are acting out – a sulky eight-year-old, a belligerent teenager, a hurt little boy or girl. When the adult verbally or physically attacks the child, it is not unlike a little boy or girl in a big body 'bullying' the real child.

Check it out. Tune in to CSPAN and watch the political debates, talks and speeches. The politicians rant, rave, call names, say mean, unkind things. Watch their facial expressions. That will indicate the age they are acting out. I find it disconcerting to see our 'leaders' spend so much of their time running the country from this childhood emotional state. On the flip side, another interesting dynamic is when human beings are being intimate, such as a grown man holding a baby and making cooing sounds. Again, human beings will revert to an earlier emotional state – where it was safe to be intimate, if you will; to be vulnerable. It is fascinating to see our adult behavior is so often an extension of our childhood.

BOUNDARIES

Boundaries are often vague. There's a lot of confusion about boundaries. You may have heard about studies where fish are placed in an aquarium, where they swim throughout the entire tank. Then a clear glass partition is placed in the middle of the tank, splitting it into two separate tanks. The fish will initially bump against the glass, as they are used to swimming the entire tank. But soon they stop, having adjusted to the tank's smaller size. Once that behavior pattern is established, the glass partition is removed. The fish don't seem to notice. They stay in the area to which they became accustomed, swimming in only half the tank. They never cross the line again. Their boundaries have been determined.

I can remember as a boy in Kansas catching grasshoppers. We'd gather them up and put them in jars with holes poked in the lids. We'd sit and watch them as they beat against the lid, jumping and jumping and jumping to get out, but of course the lid kept them in. After a time the grasshoppers would stop jumping and striking the lid of the jar. They would just sit at the bottom of the jar. Even when we opened the lids, the grasshoppers would not attempt to jump out. We would have to tip the jars over and pour the grasshoppers out. They had determined the boundaries. They learned, quite literally, how high they could jump.

To train an elephant is not a difficult thing. When the elephant is young, the trainer wraps a huge chain around its leg. The elephant must lug this chain around, a chain that limits just where it can go. The elephant learns it cannot wander off, cannot leave its place. By the time that elephant is fully-grown, the chain is no longer needed. The trainer can simply tie a lightweight cord around the elephant's leg. As long as the elephant feels something around its leg, it will not wander. It knows the rules and the limitations.

I don't think humans are much different. Psychiatrists tell us by the time a child is seven to nine years old, all the beliefs, patterns and standards are in place. At that time, whatever fundamental boundaries that have been established are firmly in place. Their behaviors reflect the boundaries that have been established. Does the child eat all vegetables or just some? When he's hurt, does he run into the house crying, or is he stoic? And where is he in the area of trust? Does he trust Mom and Dad, does he trust his sisters and brothers to do or not do certain things around the house? Boundaries are a fluid thing. They seem to come and go through life. People are always moving boundaries, establishing new boundaries and expanding them and discarding others. What is critical in growing up is that the child learn how to do this. When parents put in boundaries, consistency works. When they are changed, they must be explained thoroughly, so that the child understands that the boundaries are not being changed on a whim, but that there is thought and reasoning behind the change.

I have been told that there are studies that can determine, in a series of questions, the field of employment the child will eventually go into. They can determine whether the child is a caregiver, a mathematical thinker, or an artist. And many of these behaviors and characteristics are the direct result of the boundaries that they have established when they were children.

Boundaries can also give us many opportunities to invalidate others. It could be said that boundaries are what you put in place to determine what other people *cannot* do to you. Labeling creates a boundary. If you label someone as a jerk, chances are, you will always hold them in that light. You'll talk about them as if they were a jerk, you'll treat them as if they were a jerk. Dr. Wayne W. Dyer once said, "Labels negate people." Labels suppress people, they do not let people be who they are. It's very hard for us to let go of labels. People tend to hold to the labels. For instance, a man goes bankrupt in 1980. Ten years later, others may still label him when they say, "Oh yeah, I remember him. He went bankrupt. You can't trust him with money." Labels are a nasty piece of business that we lay on others. And they are very effective boundaries that can keep us out of harmony with others.

In all my years of coaching people, I have found that boundaries are what are missing from so many lives. When boundaries are unclear, life in general is unclear.

Somewhere, between the beatings and the bribes, there is an effective way to teach our children discipline, morals, ethics, and self-responsibility. Somehow there is a way to give our children boundaries. It's called communication.

CHAPTER 4

Family (or the lack thereof)

I grew up alienated by my half brothers and sisters. They were treated differently than I – they were spared the beatings and the putdowns – and that double standard stood in the way of any true closeness. I grew up thinking that it was *supposed* to be this way, that families *were* violent, that there *were* double standards, that the constant moving from place to place was a *normal* existence. I had nothing to compare my life to. I had few friends, therefore rarely saw the interactions of other families. This isolated, abusive world was my reality.

Christmas time proved to be a very difficult time in our family. The consequences of decisions I made back then are still present during the holidays. Early on, I of course believed in Santa Claus but it wasn't long before I realized that there really wasn't a Santa, that it was a myth designed to bring another element of surprise and happiness to that holiday season. I never realized the religious implications of Christmas, for it was organized around a tree and gifts at school, which somehow carried over into the home environment. I rarely recall a happy Christmas. At school, I was never able to adequately participate in the gift exchange without bringing embarrassment upon myself. In the home, another circumstance routinely took place.

The few gifts that we were given at Christmas were rarely things that we wanted or enjoyed. I now know that they did the best they could, but at the time, there was confusion between what I thought Christmas was to mean and the reality of it. Upset and violence escalated in our home around the holidays. There was more drinking, there was more yelling, there were more beatings; yet, the holiday was supposed to be a time of celebration. I know today that this type of behavior was not relegated to just my home environment, in fact, evidence today points to the holidays as one of the most stressful times of the year. Household violence *does* increase. Suicides *do* increase. Alcohol abuse *does* increase during this time. But I didn't know any of this, I just thought it was confined to our home. One good thing that carries over even today is my enjoyment of Christmas music. There was always an abundance of music at Christmas and I loved it all. For years my family teased me and grew weary of the Christmas music I invariably started playing on Thanksgiving Day through New Years Day. I had not a clue for the longest time why I had this behavior pattern. I would continue it even to the mild frustration of my family members. I think that I found happiness in the music and it was how I offset the trauma that routinely occurred during the holiday season. The music kept me grounded, created for me a semblance of home, celebration, and happiness that I never had in all the moves from town to town.

ADOLESCENCE

We finally ended up in Fort Dodge, Kansas. We were close to Dodge City once again. By now my grandparents had retired from the farm and had moved to Dodge City, and I was able to see them again. My grandma was still my hero – having saved me from the turkey – so being with her again was, to me, like going to heaven. I started eighth grade near my grandparents and in yet another school.

I had my first girlfriend in eighth grade. I'd found employment, at seventy-five cents an hour on a farm. The farmer's daughter and I were attracted to each other. One time, all my brothers, sisters, my new girlfriend and I went to the movies. During the movie, she and I held hands. When we got home, one of my sisters told my parents what I had done, and I was severely punished. I was told that what I had done was evil. This threw me into a state of confusion. I had seen other boys and girls holding hands and had assumed that there was nothing wrong in it. As a young adolescent, with hormones kicking in, the issue of sexuality became a minefield for me. I was confounded. I could not figure out what was right or wrong.

Unbeknownst to me, during my early childhood years, I had received conflicting messages about men, women and relationships. Given the environment I was in, I already unknowingly made several decisions from the interactions I had seen and heard between my mother and Vic. I didn't yet realize that the seeds of jealousy had been planted, the seeds of mistrust of women were planted, and this brief upset over holding a girl's hand was just one more piece of confusion added to the mix. Little did I know it would come back to haunt me with a great deal of pain.

Meanwhile, life was moving on and I attempted to live what I thought was a normal life. For my thirteenth birthday, I wanted a party. I still didn't have many friends, but I had figured that every kid loves a party, so every kid would come. My mother was excited; I'd never had a party before. We planned and prepared and I personally invited everyone in my class to come at one o'clock on Saturday afternoon. Our house was run-down, like always, so we set up the party outdoors. It was a beautiful June day. We tied balloons to the trees and made a long table from plywood. There was cake and ice cream and watermelon. I was incredibly excited, as were my brothers and sisters, who themselves had never had a party. They probably thought the party was as much for them as it was for me. One o'clock came and went. No one had arrived. I rationalized that maybe everyone was running late, but after almost two hours of rationalization, I finally let the truth in. Nobody was coming to my party. I suppose that somewhere in my subconscious I knew that would happen, but the harsh reality on that sunny June day was painful. It reminded me that I was not worth being friends with, that I was a loser.

By now the term 'loser' included much more than it did when I was younger. Now 'loser' meant that I was unworthy, that I was unattractive, that people did not really want to be around me, under any circumstance. I began to experience true loneliness. I'd been there many times before, but at this particular stage of life, I somehow thought that by my teenage years something would change, that by moving into manhood, I would somehow throw away all the pain of childhood and magically become something more. Throughout history, cultures have had initiation rites for young boys where they actually welcomed the boy into the tribe as a new man; where they actually did bring him to fruition, when there really was a delineation between childhood and manhood. It was a heavy burden at this stage of life to be known as a loser. It was a burden I would carry long into my adult years.

I now had a lifelong history of being invalidated by various circumstances, not only in my own home, but also in the outside world. It was a terrible blow that lasted many years. I was probably in my late thirties before I attempted to throw another party. Now that one was a wonderful success, yet I still retained the emotional fear of failure, the emotional trauma of being a loser and the rebuke I had learned at my first party to which no one came.

Everything in our mind is wired together. We have endless memories, emotions, feelings, sounds, odors, stored in our minds and they can all be accessed at any time with a particular incident. Even today, if I were to have a party, I would still remember the results of my first attempt at entertaining others, despite my adult knowledge that the party would be a success. These things never go away. We can manage them, we can make our peace with them, embrace them, if you will, but it isn't ever going to go away. When we are at peace with an issue, it means a new beginning. But the memory always lies in wait, ready to be activated by some new circumstance. We will explore this phenomenon in more detail later. Suffice it to say, I tucked the failed party into my memory banks and added it to my list of transgressions, those things that made me a loser, and packed them into a box with my tattered clothes as we once again prepared to move.

DECISION

I had worked at jobs since I was eight years old, and I helped the family with my earnings. I helped buy groceries, and contributed to the clothing allowance. Soon came the day that we had to move yet again. By now I had begun to see what a toll the constant relocating had taken on me. I vowed that this would be the last move, that once we got to this new town, when the family moved, for surely they would, I would not go with them. I would stay where I was. Vic took my meager savings and moved our family to a small town in Missouri, where I would have one last chance to make a team.

In all these years I had still never made a team. I still tried out, and I always ended up embarrassed. But I never quit trying. By the time we moved back to Missouri, I had a little more confidence in myself. I was still a poor student, but now I was beginning to learn how to handle myself, how to cope with the rest of the world. I know now that my number one defense in those days was my arrogance, a self-defense coping mechanism. At the time, however, I didn't see myself as arrogant.

Arrogance is fear-based, and I had endless fears. When I was confronted, I would use arrogance as a defense, an attempt to be all those things that I wasn't. This was how I survived, how I coped: by going on the offense, by attacking before I was attacked. I would attempt to be brave, to stand taller, to look people in the eye. I would attempt to be courageous and pretend that I wasn't afraid of anything. As it carried over into my adult life, it served a purpose. It helped me through difficult times, yet at the same time (though I didn't know it) it shut many doors. When I finally became aware of the deadly cost of arrogance, I realized that, while I could never jettison the fear, that it was part of me, I knew I could learn to manage it. When I am mindful of my arrogance, it's very powerful and gives me a lot of insight and depth to bring to a situation. When I forget, it causes me, as it always did, pain. That is especially true today, because I can identify it instantly. Knowing that we are simply mirrors of each other, you can easily understand when I recognize arrogance in another person, what makes it possible for me to recognize it, is my own arrogance. When I recognize it in another person, I have to be mindful to stay detached, to keep from going to my past memories or reactions. I know that if I am not mindful, my own arrogance can come out with a flourish, alive and well, and as always cause damage. It damages not only the person I am interacting with, it damages me, too, since it is simply an attack on both of us.

My arrogance was alive and well when I arrived in one more town. We came to that small town in the early summer of 1956. I was committed to staying where I was; I was not going to switch towns and schools ever again. Since I was going to complete high school here, I had an even deeper conviction to get on a team. I was old enough to really see what a profound influence sports had on a boy's life. I craved that affirmation and support as much as I craved to be free of the beatings and the putdowns.

I had to choose a sport that I could practice by myself, that I could learn in my own private world. I chose basketball. I was able to find a used basketball hoop. I made a backdrop from scrap wood and cut down a slim tree, prepped it and anchored it in the ground.

Then I practiced. And I practiced. And I practiced. I poured my heart and soul – my very being – into my practice. It was an obsession. I believed that basketball would be my salvation. I would practice in the mud, I would practice in the moonlight. It didn't make any difference to me. I was still desperate; life had not changed.

Just as always, we lived on the poor side of town. We had a few acres, but there was no running water. We boiled water in a huge cauldron outside where my mother would wash our clothes with an old wringer washer outside. Just as always, Vic did not not hold down a job. I had a different ethic. I worked hard and I worked well and soon acquired a reputation among the neighbors for being a good worker, reliable and competent.

I had a variety of jobs during my high school years. This particular summer I picked strawberries for eight cents per quart, and dug postholes in the rocky Missouri soil for fifty cents an hour. I also worked in the hay fields, stacking hay bales on a truck and unloading them at the barn, all for one or two cents per bale. I worked on an average of four to six hours a day, leaving me a bit of free time. So I read. It was one of the things I loved the most. The traveling bookmobile was my savior that summer.

Finally summer ended and I started my high school years in another new school. I was one of only one hundred students in the entire school. Just as always, I shuffled in, head down, and sat in the back of the classroom. Just as always, I was the new kid. I kept my mouth shut. From my own little island in the back of the class, I observed the interactions of my classmates; I determined that day who the popular kids were, who was in, who was out. I was so good at watching people that I could tell in the first hour who the smart kids were and who was affluent.

By now the family had acquired a pig, a milk cow and some chickens. We burned firewood for fuel. I was the oldest and was expected to take care of those things. My younger brothers would sometimes help, as would Vic on occasion. Primarily, though, those chores fell upon my shoulders. I think it was probably a good thing. It taught me self-reliance and self-responsibility at an early age, even if it was fear-based. In other words, "The buck stopped with me!" So I held myself responsible for my chores, but once they were done, I moved on to something that was truly urgent: basketball practice.

I practiced basketball. I'd go out in the evening and practice well into the night. With each shot, I dreamed of being a hero again, of making the winning shot, of the cheers and adulation of the crowd and my teammates. I dreamed of a pretty cheerleader hugging me and kissing my sweaty face, and I dreamed of the smile on the coach's face and the team running up to hoist me on their shoulders for winning the game.

It seemed to me that basketball was my hope, my desperation, my obsession. Basketball was my only way out of the prison that was my life. It would bring me friends. If I were a basketball star, people might think I was worthy of their friendship, even though I knew deep down inside that I really wasn't. Still, it drove me, night after night after night.

About the middle of October, basketball tryouts were announced. I thought I would surely make the team because I had practiced so hard. I had practiced on my own, though, so my skills were rather rough. After a couple of weeks, the coach announced who was on the team and who wasn't. When I was cut from the ninth grade team, I was devastated and sick at heart. My small world came crashing down. My home life and all the events of my childhood had left me with very low self-esteem. Now my self-label as 'loser' escalated to where I felt incredible humiliation. This had been where I was going to get to start over. This was the place where no one knew me, where I could shed my history and actually fit in. I had counted on that with my whole heart, to rescue myself from how I'd been labeled and how I saw myself all those years. But now it was even more difficult to look people in the eye, more difficult to watch the boys who made the team, given that it was such a small school and I saw every student every day. Of course, everyone knew who had made the team and who didn't. Once again, I came into ridicule. I was made to feel small. I was once more hanging my head and shuffling down the hallways. And once more I had few friends or acquaintances and those I did have were very much like me, since circumstances dictated one more time how I felt about myself.

Think of the old adage, "Birds of a feather flock together." We seek out those who are most like ourselves, people who have similar beliefs and similar lives. If you have deeply religious beliefs, you will count as your friends those people whose beliefs are most like yours. If you're an avid golfer, your friends are more likely to be golfers. This is the natural order of things. It is also one of the reasons that we feel uncomfortable when we are put into situations where we must interact with people who are not like us. This can be a major or minor issue or problem, as each person in the interaction is, unknowingly, attempting to have the other person think just like they do. Of course, that rarely happens when we interact with people whose thinking is diametrically opposed to ours. Most of us do not have the skills necessary to just listen. So even while I was hanging out with 'losers,' I was still very committed to being on a team.

MAKING THE TEAM

Fitting in by making the team

I refused to be denied. From my point of view, there still did not seem to be any other way to earn the respect and admiration of the other kids in school. I *had* to be an athlete. I *had* to be a star. This had made itself apparent from the very start of my school years. The athletes had the recognition, the respect and admiration of not only the other students, but also the teachers and townspeople. I did not have abundance in my life, nor did I have any other way of taking my place in the sun.

I was cut from a team yet again; but the coach encouraged me. He told me if I practiced a lot, I might be able to make the team next year. I summoned up my courage and ask him if I could have a basketball, a *real* ball, made of leather, even though it was specifically for indoor basketball. He gave me one, and once more I set to work practicing. I wore out four balls that next year, dribbling them on the hard dirt of my small court. I would play alone. I would practice hook shots, one after the other, time and time again. Every spare moment was spent in practicing hook shots. It paid off. When I was a senior, I made forty-one points in one game, the majority coming from my fifteen-foot hook shot. But I digress.

I was a big fellow for those times, and knew that once I made the team, I would be playing under the basket. So I practiced hook shots, and jump shots, lay-ups and free throws. I would imagine I was up against a live defense. I would run around them. I would fake them out. It was as real to me as the sky over my head. When it rained, I would use the puddles as defensive players. When it snowed, I would imagine someone's hand in my face. When I was cold, I would wear gloves. I'd smell the ball, the dirt, the air. I would imagine thousands of people cheering me on. Every shot was a chance to win or lose the state championship. Later, when I was a senior, we did go to the state championship. We lost. And even though I was the high scorer on my team, I was still a loner, I was still a loser, just as I had been when I was practicing outdoors in the heat, the rain and the snow, hearing the silent cheers of thousands of imaginary fans.

A whole year passed. It was October of my sophomore year. I was scared. But I came anyway to try out for the team, one more time. I was shocked, however, when I saw that the coach who had encouraged me, had given me basketballs to practice with, had moved away. We had a new coach. He was young; this would be his first season coaching. I knew he had heard about how bad I was; after all, he asked me how the leather ball was holding up.

During the try-outs I ran faster than I ever had. I dove for absolutely every loose ball; I did everything I could to deny my opponent the ball. I played like it was my last chance, and indeed, it was. The sweat would run into my eyes where it would burn, but I wouldn't stop. I wouldn't let anyone see me breathe hard. I would come in early and stay late. I would memorize the plays at night. I would go home and practice on my dirt court. To everyone else it was a game, but to me it was my life. It was an obsession. I was driven by all my fears and past failures, and my huge desire to be part of a team.

When I was told I was on the "B" team and that I was to be a starter, I don't recall up to that point having a happier moment in my life.

I can still recall that magical day. It didn't matter that the "B" team consisted of mostly every tenth grade boy in the school; it didn't matter that there were just twenty-five students in the entire class. What mattered was that I was on a TEAM. I had a uniform! I would wear the school colors. I was given a purpose; I was given something to look forward to. For the next several months, and the first time ever for me, I was going to get to play real games. Finally, I was given the chance to see if what I had dreamed of could come true. *I was on a team!*

Whether we realize it or not, we are all on teams. In some way, we are connected to others and work with each other to accomplish whatever needs to be done. And until I made that "B" squad, I had never before felt anything like the sense of belonging that suddenly filled me. I was ecstatic! I shivered with excitement and adrenaline; I could hardly speak!

My mother was thrilled. She knew how much it meant to me to be a member of a team. She had worried and prayed over me for so long – finally her prayers were answered. I had achieved my dream, despite all the failures at school and at home.

Vic treated the news with little regard. He was true to form when he made some derogatory comment. For the first time ever, his words had no effect. I was too happy to let him get me down. I was a winner this day. I was on top of the world and his comments failed to touch me as I once more headed outside to practice.

With my acceptance to the team, I practiced even harder. For the other boys, basketball was a game, something to do, a way to pass the time. But for me it was real life. This was where my life was. It wasn't about family, church, school or grades. All I knew was that I needed to play basketball and I needed to excel.

For the first time, I had a coach; someone who took the time to work with me. I was amazed that someone would actually pull me aside and teach me how to shoot, dribble, and pass. I'd never had such an experience. I was astounded that there was training and discipline without anger and violence.

Soon we played our first game, and I was a starter! It was a thrill to be out on the floor, running with my teammates, passing and driving the ball up and down the floor. I played well. And I kept playing well. Soon, I was promoted to the "A" team as a substitute. I was a bench warmer, but that didn't matter. I was on the team.

My big chance came mid-season. Most of the starters had fouled out. I was the last eligible player on the bench. With seconds left in the game, coach came to me and said, "Elliott, I'm going to send you in. Now, whatever you do, DON'T SHOOT THE BALL!"

It was the wrong thing to say to me. The coach didn't realize that I had waited my whole life for this moment. It was the moment I had dreamed of, the opportunity that had driven me for many years. I ran out to the floor. Then, as if preordained, I got possession of the ball. The clock was running out. I looked around, recognized that I had the shot, and with coach screaming from the sidelines, "DON'T SHOOT THE BALL," I took aim and let fly. I shot the ball. It hung in the air, the room suddenly silent as the ball arced gracefully over the heads of the players. Swoosh! Nothing but net! I made the basket! It was just as I had imagined it would be. The crowd was a wall of cheers and adulation. My teammates were jumping and screaming and ran to hoist me on their shoulders. Pretty cheerleaders hung on my neck and kissed my not-so-sweaty face. Coach even forgave my disobedience. I was a hero. For the third time ever, I was really a hero and this time it was *not* from being rescued from a turkey and it *wasn't* from fighting a fire.

The next day at school, I noticed a change. Suddenly everyone was friendlier. The teachers were friendlier; the girls were definitely friendlier. Boys who had hardly spoken to me were now anxious to befriend me. I was treated well, not just by the students, but also by the teachers. I found my sense of humor and began to use it in the classroom. Now I had permission to cut up and be a class clown. My behavior was not just accepted, it was encouraged. All because of a *circumstance* known as basketball.

My skill at basketball brought me into the world I had always dreamed of. Basketball became my whole reason for living. Unknowingly though, I now brought my arrogance into my basketball playing. I was used to using arrogance as a defense mechanism; now it altered to the point where I literally went on the attack with it. Since I had very few places in my life to shine and basketball was the key for me, I started developing an attitude of "I'm better than you" on the court. It was good news and bad news. It helped drive me to excel, to be accepted, but it also led me to become full of myself. The saddest day of the year was the day of the last game. When the season ended, I had nothing to look forward to, from March to late the next fall. This was probably the first recollection that I truly have an inkling of how circumstances dictated how I felt about myself. There was no other area of my life where I received recognition and acknowledgment. From the time I was a youngster, I knew that when one did good things, one was praised; when one did bad things, one was rejected. Of course while not realizing it at the time, each individual has standards of what's right and what's wrong, determined by their value system. It depends on whose environment you're in, whether you'll be made right or wrong for any action you might take. I had figured out that the circumstance of playing basketball and being a star was the only way I could really feel good about myself. The rest of the time, for the most part, I went back to my self-image, my poor self-esteem – ever the 'loser.' There was nothing else that made me stand out, stand above the rest, to be recognized. But I knew I could not rely on my circumstance as a basketball player to carry me through the rest of my life.

In later years, I came to recognize that most people, most of the time, without conscious thought, let the quality of their life be determined by their circumstances. So if they have a good day at work (circumstances went well) and if their actions are consistent with what others demand of them, they feel good about themselves. If the day is somehow inconsistent with what was demanded and expected of them, it's usually taken personally in the form of "something is wrong with me." People, for the most part, seem to be engaged in having their lives be acceptable to someone else's standards. This can look like attempting to be recognized by others, to please others simply to feel better about themselves. And since circumstances are ever changing – good times, bad times – there is ample opportunity to be invalidated by one's circumstances.

Things settled back into the old routine at both school and home. I worked hard at home and for the farmers, but basketball still dominated my life. I still went out every evening after chores and practiced. My obsession continued, as I was now able to hold my head up in that environment.

There was a church nearby, so we attended services sporadically. Growing up, as we moved from town to town, mother would enroll us in summer bible schools and we would often attend Sunday school. Mother was a churchgoer and Vic never stepped foot in a church, so these were confusing times for me. Each parish had its own style; some were open and friendly, some were closed and prim. Some ministers seemed kind and benign while others seemed wild and scary. Even though I was shabbily dressed and my English was poor, I held my head high. There were other boys that attended church and they knew my name from basketball. They respected me. It was not the sermons, or the scripture that brought me to church, it was those boys. I was included in that rarified environment of the athlete, and basketball was our common ground. Church became a 'must' for me, as it was there that I received emotional indulgence from the other boys.

I got a job the summer prior to my junior year of high school. I got to milk cows. There was just one problem: I had to walk one and a half miles each way, twice a day. Our family had only one vehicle and usually, either Mother or Vic was using it. Sometimes I got lucky and hitched a ride.

I'd get up at five a.m., walk over, find the cows, then get them to the barn, where I hand-milked five of them while an old, beat-up milking machine milked another two cows. The job paid a dollar and a quarter a day; I was fortunate to have this job for almost a full year.

When I had late basketball practice or a game, my brother, Jim, would do my job for half my daily rate. It was a great help for both of us, since we both desperately needed the money. In today's world, I find it difficult to find a teenager who will mow my lawn. It seems most children today have too many choices, not enough discipline, far too many activities, and parents who would rather be a 'buddy' than a parent teaching discipline, boundaries and a work ethic.

When I was a junior, I made the first string, the "A" team. My name made it into the papers and I got headlines as my basketball career took off. Now I was recognized, a necessary ingredient for someone who needed favorable circumstances for validation.

I kept every statistic imaginable, for every game, every year. I'd go back in my files to remind myself how well I'd done. This wasn't a game for me; this was salvation. This was how I made it; how I recovered my self-esteem. This is how I held my head up when I wore shoes with holes in them and old clothes, and lived on the other side of the tracks. This was how I got to be a hero, how I got to be accepted.

My mother worked nights in a hospital. She would bring home the local paper, plus one from the 'big city' nearby. By seven-thirty in the morning, I would have read about my exploits and that of my team. Once, after I had scored thirty-three points in a game, one of the papers compared me to the great basketball star, Wilt Chamberlain. Heady stuff, and I must say, I thrived on it, as did my arrogance.

Basketball was my light and my salvation. My reward for putting up with all the stuff I didn't like, all the prices I'd paid over the years. One thing that came back to haunt me later was that I thought I deserved all the praise, all the attention. I felt that life owed me something if I performed, and was finally paying its debt to me. I carried that pattern into areas of my life later on. Meanwhile, even in the midst of all my family troubles, my grades improved somewhat, I was definitely more popular, and sometimes I would even get to go out on a date.

LIFE GOES ON

The family life continued much as it always had. While we did not have running water, we did have electricity this time, and finally got the luxury of a beat-up black and white television. I can still recall one program that fascinated me was Art Linkletter's *Queen For A Day*. It was a simple program. They would have three mothers brought in from around the country. Art would interview them and they would tell some of the saddest and most pathetic stories I had ever heard. Then the audience would cheer for the most dramatic story, or in my opinion, the worst story. They even had an applause meter, so they would know who won. So here were these women, always mothers, telling these horrific stories to the delight of the audience. The winner would get a felt cape, a tinsel crown and scepter, and prizes like washers and refrigerators. While these prizes might have been great conveniences, I was always amazed that the women would never get a vacation or a day off, or anything that might make life a little more fun. We seem to live in a culture that has great tolerance for suffering. Programs like this actually glorify suffering. This is a common trait among humans. We are drawn to observe suffering; we actually feed on the suffering of others. Public hangings, beheadings and burnings entertained man in the Dark and Middle Ages. Today it's Jerry Springer, his imitators, and the tabloids. We slow down at the scenes of auto accidents, looking for the victims, looking for something gory to revile yet compel us. For me it was *Queen For A Day*.

I wrote to Art Linkletter many times. I felt that if my mother could get on the show, her story would be a winner. We had far worse stories in our household than anything I ever heard on TV. We never did hear from Art, my mother never became Queen for a day, and life just went on.

GROWING UP

The summer before my senior year, I just knew I had to make money. There were girls I wanted to date, and that cost money. I wanted a class ring. That cost money, too. There was the senior class picture, the senior class trip, and of course, I needed a suit for graduation. This was an enormous load for me. I had no financial support from my family; in fact, I had been contributing to the family budget for several years. I knew I would get very little, if any, work during the school year.

Scientists had finally developed hybrid tomatoes. I was excited. I could see an income from growing and selling my tomatoes. So I scraped together a few dollars and hired a neighbor to come plow a half-acre of ground. I prepared the soil, then bought five thousand tomato plants. Looking back, I can't believe that I had the courage and the audacity to try this without any real farming background. But the neighbor who plowed the field encouraged me. He and his family grew strawberries and he told me that when my crop came in, I could go with his boys to sell the produce. This excited me to no end.

I worked very hard that summer. I had to carry water up to the field from a well at the bottom of the hill. The first mistake I made was in fertilizer. I didn't know that in those days the fertilizer would burn the tender young plants. The stalks of the plants shriveled up, turned brown and fell over. I lost a third of my plants to fertilizer burn. I replaced the plants and learned another valuable lesson.

All summer I worked that field. Every day I weeded and watered, picked bugs and prayed for a successful crop. I practically lived in that field. My work paid off. I had an enormous crop of the biggest tomatoes I had ever seen.

My neighbor stayed true to his word. His sons loaded up their crop of strawberries, peaches, apples, and green beans, and I with my tomatoes joined them as we went from town to town selling our produce for whatever we could get. At nicer homes, we charged a little more than at homes in poorer neighborhoods. We'd drive down the street, sometimes ringing a bell to attract attention. At noon every day, we'd head to the edge of town to inspect our produce. After a morning of peddling, some of the tomatoes would be too soft to sell, some of the peaches would be bruised, and some of the beans would be broken. We would regroup and freshen our displays and go back for more sales in the afternoon.

We did that for about three weeks during the harvest. When the dust settled and I counted my earnings, I discovered that not only did I *not* make a profit, I had barely broken even. That first summer of hybrid tomatoes was popular. You could literally throw a tomato out the window and it would grow all the way to the sky. Everyone had tomatoes. I could hardly give them away. This was my first real business venture. I had made an investment and worked hard, yet I did not become rich.

I still have a keen interest in gardening, but I never again attempted to make money at it. I did learn, however, what it was like to work hard. I learned about support from my neighbor. I learned how to sell (a skill I *have* used for many years). It all started in that tomato patch where I learned first hand how to talk to people, how to sell, how to ask them for money and how to talk about my product. I'm sure I was rough, but it was a beginning. I still cherish the experience I got that summer.

SENIOR YEAR

I realized that summer that I needed to look ahead to the future. I had grown up wanting nothing more than to finish high school and move out of that violent atmosphere, away from the man who called himself my father. My mother had never finished high school and Vic barely finished eighth grade. I was going to be the first person in my family to graduate from high school. This was a dream my mother held in high esteem, for she knew that an education could take me away from the pain, the hurt, the desolation of my home life.

Entering my senior year, I was confused and uncertain. Where I would go and what I would do were still unresolved issues to be determined. What would make me happy? What could I accomplish in my life? There was certainly no money for college, and though I was a good player, with my poor grades I doubted that I could get a scholarship. By then, though, I knew I had to go to college. My confidence grew with my hunger to excel and soon basketball wasn't enough. I took up other challenges.

I tried out for the senior play. To my surprise, I was selected! It was wonderful. Being in the play was like being on another team. Imagine my surprise when on Award Day, my name was called out. I had won the "Actor Achievement Award." I credit this win to my experience on the basketball team. It was out of my growing confidence that I even had the courage to try out. Then life took another turn.

In the winter of 1959, my senior year, my parents moved back to Kansas. True to my vow, I didn't go. I suppose that, legally, they could have made me go with them, but by that time I had become quite independent. They left without me. I lived alone for a short time, then I began to live with teammates. We were very close, playing basketball together, but it was a bit of a challenge living around, so to speak. Wherever I stayed I was mindful of the rules and always contributed. Even so, one mother made me move out. I thought it was because I was getting bigger newspaper headlines than her son. Evidently, she was jealous so she made me move. I was hurt badly at the time. They were affluent, with a big house and lots of room. I felt like I was being sent out into the cold, snowy night again, to find a big stick, and it invoked those memories of being a loser. I was being punished, being sent away, simply for excelling in basketball. I never understood it then, but now I can see that it was probably my growing arrogance that led to my dismissal as a houseguest.

After several months, I received a call. Mom and Vic were moving back. Despite the hardships I'd endured, I was disappointed to hear that they were coming back to town. I reluctantly moved back home. I knew it meant more violence and harsh treatment. Even though moving around from house to house was hard, it was an adventure for this teenage boy without parents. All in all, I had grown stronger. Playing on a team, being part of a team was more important to me. I had, through basketball, experienced more of a feeling of family than I did in my own home. When I was with my team, I was a member of something great. We communicated. We worked together. We made things happen. My basketball team was more of a family to me than the people with whom I shared a name. Nevertheless, I moved back into that hostile family environment.

It had been some time since Vic had beaten me. I was rarely home, busy with school, work, and basketball, so opportunities for beatings were rare. One evening I came home late to find Vic holding a gun on my mother, threatening her once again. As it turned out, it was the *last* time Vic threatened her.

Over the years I had dreamed of being big enough and strong enough to make Vic be good to my mother and me. I wanted to stop his abuses and make him respect us. Suddenly, in that moment, all those emotions, all those hurts and angers boiled to the surface. I was no longer the scared little boy who had been battered into submission. No longer would I stand for the whipping and the punching. My body was strong and hard from work on the farms and from basketball practice. As I saw my mother standing in mortal fear, all logical thought fled from my mind. A surge of anger overtook me and in a blur of rage, I ran into the house, grabbed Vic and dragged him out the door.

I don't remember the next few moments. I was blind with fury as I punched him, kicked him, tore at him with all the vengeance in my scarred and wounded soul. And I kept on punching him, I kept on kicking him, I kept on beating him. I wanted to destroy him, to make him feel as my mother and I had felt for so many years. For every blow he had given me, I returned it with anger, hurt, and rage.

I can still remember my mother's hands pulling me off him. She knew with this dramatic turn of events our lives would change forever. The next morning, Vic announced that he was leaving. I was thrilled and scared to see him go, and so was my mother who was still trying to make sense of the previous night's events. She had never had the courage to kick him out or leave him. The last time I saw him alive, he was sober. He apologized profoundly for his abuse, leaving me emotionally confused. He packed his belongings and left that day. We never saw him or heard from him again. Nor did we ever hear anything about him while he was alive.

Several years later, I received a call from a hospital. I was told that Vic had died. He'd died sober. All I could think at the time was, "How strange…"

During these years and for many years to come, whenever I saw or heard someone who reminded me of Vic, instantly my fear would come back, my heart would race and my palms would sweat. I finally did complete this part of my life, but it would take many years and a lot of hard work to overcome Vic's horrible abuses.

It was a strange feeling when Vic first left. Suddenly the fear was gone; the cloud that hung over the household suddenly lifted. It was as if the sun finally shone for the first time. It was an incredible sense of freedom. I didn't have to worry about my mother and I didn't have to worry about myself.

It did leave a new burden, however. Even though he'd gotten fired from every job he ever had, even though he drank away most of what he did earn, Vic did, from time to time, contribute to the family funds. Now I had to work even harder.

One of my jobs during high school was weekend work in a hatchery. One day I was walking down a long chicken house, between the rows of cages. Suddenly, from behind, I heard a turkey gobbling and approaching rapidly. Without any thought, without looking back, I bolted and ran. After a few steps, I heard laughter from a group of men standing nearby. Turning around, I saw nothing more than a small turkey. I now know the reason for my reaction. If you'll remember, a turkey attacked me when I was very small. That memory, etched into my very being, came to light that day in the chicken house. When I heard the gobbling, I was sent back in time emotionally, to age five, where the fear still lived. This is another example of how patterns, notions and beliefs are formed; unknowingly, without plan on our part. You can see how the events of our childhood dictate how we react to all situations, how our past and our future are intertwined through these events. It was so in my life, and it is so in yours.

It was the spring of my senior year. The season was almost over, in fact, it was the last game of the regular season. I had been the leading scorer for two years now. True to form, I took the last shot of the game for the final points and the victory. But this time I missed the shot and we lost the game. I went to the Dairy Queen, our local hangout, after the game. I felt bad. People came by, saying things like, "I'm glad I didn't have to make that shot," and, "too bad you missed." There were many remarks. Most were kind, some were unkind. All I know is that I felt really, really bad. Little did I know that this incident hooked up with my past, fed into my 'loser' label and that I had already formed those patterns, notions and beliefs into rules, emotions, and feelings that would challenge me some twenty years later.

The small town in Missouri where I completed high school was a town that held strong attitudes. I didn't realize it at the time, but the town, generally speaking, was bigoted. At the town limits posted on both sides of the highway that ran through town hung signs that read, "Coloreds Don't Stop Here." I remember seeing those signs and being shocked. I did not know much about black people. I had never read anything, and I hadn't heard much. All I had to go on was my own experience. I had been treated well by the few black people I'd met. My limited contact showed me that the blacks I had known were kind, generous, and compassionate. I was really confused. Once, when I tried to bring up the subject with my basketball teammates, I was jeered, hooted at and made wrong. They teased me and called me names. And these were my friends! So I shut up about it. I did know how to keep my mouth shut. Vic taught me that. Here I was, struggling to figure out this huge chasm between my culture and my experiences. Rather than create waves, which would surely have ended with me on the receiving end of violence, I simply ignored my own questions and kept quiet. This dilemma squashed my enthusiasm for defending a cause with which I was not intimate, defending people I did not know. I had no black friends at the time, indeed, hadn't even seen a black person for years and years. I just remember feeling that something wasn't right. I could not assimilated cultural traditions with my personal notions, so I concentrated on finishing the basketball season and work.

Being poor, I was always on the lookout for work opportunities. Just a few weeks prior to graduation, Mom, who was a nurse's aide in a hospital some eight miles from home, got me a job in the hospital for seven nights straight. The patient had wanted a practical nurse, but none were available. So, my mother talked her supervisor into letting me sit up all night with the patient. Mom would check in on me, since she worked the night shift. This was my first opportunity to really see how hard my mother worked, how much she really knew. Although she was just a nurse's aide who'd never completed high school, she had so much practical knowledge that she was the one who would train the new registered nurses who had book knowledge, though not the work experience. I saw her compassion for the ill, how the patients she cared for appreciated her. I saw her commitment to their well being. I probably came to love and respect my mother more in those few nights than at any other time in our relationship.

Today my mother is living in a nursing home of her choice in Alaska, and is well cared-for. Her knowledge is still serving her well. She makes friends easily and is proud that she is still taking care of herself. Even now, she occasionally reminds me of the time we 'worked together.'

I was very fortunate those seven nights. I earned roughly two dollars an hour. It was where the majority of the money came from for my graduation suit, class ring and all the other things a high school senior wants and needs. I was very prudent with my money. After giving Mama a portion, I would save some. Money was so scarce that during the last two years of high school, I got a job mopping the cafeteria floors so I could eat for free. I put up with a lot of teasing. Every kid and teacher in school saw me working while they were taking a break or having fun. For me it was classes, work, then more classes. My work ethic carried over to college. There I would wash dishes in exchange for lunch. Over time, it seemed that I had become immune to the ribbing. But of course, this reminder of poverty simply added to all the other issues and insecurities I already had.

This was the same time in my life that I would buy used shoes at the shoe store. I can remember re-gluing the soles of my shoes, or tying straps of inner tube around them to hold them together. While all these simple memories seem sad, they helped give me the courage to keep looking ahead, not back.

I graduated in the spring of 1960. I was no closer to having a life's goal than I had been the previous fall. All I knew was that I needed to make money; I needed to support the family, and I needed an opportunity. My friend James said we could accompany his father to the oil fields in west Kansas. So I borrowed fifty dollars from the bank (a favor because I was a graduating senior) and joined James and his dad in an old Ford to head out west to work.

CHAPTER 5

Communication

I went to the dictionary to read the definition of "communication." It was there that I found an entire page of words containing the root word, *commune*. Commune means to 'have an intimate exchange or discussion, feel close to, in touch with…' "Communication" is defined as 'shared possession, common participation; a similarity; a sharing.' So when we communicate, we share, we exchange ideas, we discuss, we may feel close to others, and in touch with intimacy.

Communication is essential for our very existence. Good relationships actually improve our health. When we have clear communication with those we love, we can accomplish more, we can take care of ourselves and each other better. For communication to be clear, we must listen with our hearts. We must hear the words and see the actions of those we love. We must listen deeply and fully to the communication. For if we do not, the words and hopes of our loved ones are lost on the wind. And if we cannot hear others, who will listen to us?

Many years ago, I took advantage of an opportunity to meet and hear retired Navy Commander Gerald Coffee deliver a profound speech regarding communication. I'd like to share my version of his story with you:

Jerry was flying back to his aircraft carrier after a mission in war-torn Vietnam. Just minutes from touchdown, and just hours before he was to leave for a well earned R&R, his plane was struck by a missile. Jerry and his co-pilot ejected and fell with the debris of the downed plane into the ocean. After his parachute had opened and he was drifting to earth, he saw two motor launches approaching them from the shore. As he went into the water, he saw that the personnel in the launch nearing his co-pilot were shooting at him. It would not be until seven years later that Commander Coffee found out that his co-pilot had indeed been killed.

Jerry, however, was picked up, loaded onto the back of an old truck and taken to a POW camp behind North Vietnamese lines. As I recall, he said the journey took two or three days, winding through the jungle from village to village. The truck would stop at each village and the people would come and throw rotten vegetables and other trash, cursing and spitting on him. He was finally brought to an old French prison with thick stone walls, the cells lining all four sides of a center courtyard. His prison mates were all like him: downed flyers.

Jerry had been badly injured when his plane was shot down; he had several broken bones and was in very poor shape by the time he received medical attention. Days later, he was taken out of his cell for his first shower. As he stood under the rusty water dripping from an ancient faucet, he looked up to a small patch of sunlight streaming through a tiny window far above him. He'd been praying all these days for God to give him those last moments before the crash; to let him have another chance. And as he looked at that small patch of sunlight, he again repeated the prayer. Soon, though, his eyes wandered down the wall. In front of him he saw the message that would change his entire view of the situation. On that wall, scratched in by another prisoner were the words, "Smile. You're on Candid Camera." At that moment, Jerry said he realized that he was offering up a futile prayer, and that he had to change his attitude.

Commander Coffee was a prisoner for seven years. He was among the longest-held prisoners of the Vietnam conflict. For the most part, those seven years were spent inside his tiny cell. Sometimes he was taken into the exercise yard to chop wood and perform other chores. Sometimes he was taken for interrogation, a process of torture, beatings and abuse. He was never allowed to speak to the other prisoners, nor were they allowed to speak with him. The Vietcong guards maintained a strict rule of silence.

But American soldiers are taught a form of code that uses a series of taps. And this is what those brave warriors did. They used the code, tapping out their thoughts and news from the outside. Without ever speaking aloud, the prisoners were able to communicate, to talk to each other. They tapped out messages on the stone walls of the prison. But it didn't stop there. They used every activity as an opportunity to communicate. When they chopped wood, they chopped in code. Even clearing the throat or a cough held a message.

Jerry said that early on he realized, that to stay alive, he had to commit to communicate. During those seven years, Jerry learned several foreign languages, simply by listening to them. He learned French, Russian, and Vietnamese. He memorized poetry and can recite for days. Jerry told us that those men who were healthy enough but did not survive the prison camp were those that gave up on communicating. They isolated themselves and fed into the torture of silence. The men who survived were the ones who kept communication open at all costs.

By age 10, love, trust and self esteem principles have been determined

There were humorous times, too. Jerry recalls a day when a newly-downed pilot tapped out, "The Green Bay Packers won the first Superbowl?" Jerry tapped back, "What's a Superbowl?" He'd been so long in prison he had no clue about the event.

Jerry looks back at those seven years as the most influential and empowering in his entire life. In that old French prison in the jungles of Vietnam, Jerry learned forgiveness; he'd learned foreign languages and learned how to express himself. He said he came back a better person, a better father, a better husband and a better family man. He learned that he was free, even if he was in a small cell cut off from the world. He was free because he could communicate with others.

PERSONALITY DEVELOPMENT

While we are born with certain personality traits, the development of that personality can be described by predictable, age-related stages, and there are endless ways to evaluate these stages. On the whole, however, in the psychiatric world, there is a general consensus:

By the time a child is a year old, he/she has developed his/her sense of trust and a sense of how safe it is to give and receive love. These aspects are determined by the child's environment during this first year. How is she treated when she cries? What type of home is it? Are people always yelling at each other? Is the home nurturing and loving? Is it safe? Is the child held and cuddled? In other words, these personality developments are a direct result of the environment.

Psychologists also tell us between the ages of one and three is when the foundation for self-esteem is set in place or not. Again, this is in direct proportion to the child's environment. Is the child ridiculed? Is the child put down? How is the child corrected? What is the quality of the interaction? Is the child spanked? Is the child yelled at? These are all components to the foundation for self-esteem. The child's life can be altered, patched, reinforced, even dismantled and put back together again, but through it all is this foundation that was laid by the age of three.

By the time a child is seven to nine years old, psychologists tell us that the foundation of 'Self' is in place. Beliefs are in place, as are the core rules that are a result of those beliefs. A child is the product of her environment. Along with the genetic makeup, this determines how she will handle her environment. These belief systems are the basis for how the child sees her life. Why does one child become belligerent while another, in the same household and the same situation, becomes silent and withdrawn? That is the combination of genetics and environment. The fact remains that both children have been taught certain things within that household that will dictate their attitudes and behavior patterns for the remainder of their lives.

Life doesn't just run on perpetual motion once adulthood is reached. We continue to develop throughout life. How we develop, how we help our children develop, is the crux of the situation. We can choose to accept the circumstances of stages passed long ago, or we can resolve those early conflicts and put a closure to the negative messages we received as infants. I spent the early part of my adult life living in a world of arrogance to cover my low self-esteem, beliefs I had formed since childhood. I had to break them down. I had to change the behaviors and the patterns so that I could learn to communicate and be in harmony with others. I had to break down the barriers.

CHAPTER 6

Adulthood

After high school James and I found an apartment we could share and took work in the oilfields of Kansas. This was my first 'real' job. I made $2.75 an hour plus overtime. I worked as much overtime as possible and soon had enough saved to buy an old car. I still sent money home to my mother.

It felt good to be on my feet. I was helping out at home. I was contributing and even saving a few dollars, and it gave me a feeling of satisfaction and contentment. My work ethic continued to serve me well, and it was with happiness that I saw my mother's lot in life improve, too.

That fall, my mother remarried, to a retired teacher and elder in her church. He had moved in next door after building a new house. Even though he was retired and his children grown and gone, both he and my mother knew this would be a good situation for both of them. It would mean security for mother and her five children, and he would have someone to care for him, as he was aged and ill. A pleasant surprise from this union was the birth of my half-brother, Paul, with whom I am very close. With my mother's future looking bright, I was able to move on.

I saved enough money from my work in the oilfields to start college. I returned home and enrolled in a small junior college nearby. I tried out for the basketball team as a walk-on. My years of practice and obsession paid off. I was given a basketball scholarship, which allowed me to buy books, pay tuition, and get me started in college. I majored in education. I loved basketball, and I played well. I wanted to teach it to other kids. I was young and I knew I would be an excellent coach.

Imagine my excitement when I met Harold. Not only was Harold the blackest man I had ever seen, he was a much better ball player than I. He was the most popular boy in the entire junior college. He was bright, he was witty, he was handsome, and he was talented.

As I got to know Harold, he exploded my learned attitudes about blacks. For the third time in my life, I had come into contact with a different race, a different culture. I had grown up in a culture that said blacks were lazy, shiftless, dishonest and untrustworthy. The irony of these cultural attitudes and Vic's behaviors was lost on me as a child. But my experience with a black boy when I was small and again with that wonderful elderly couple had always nagged at me. Harold's presence in my life finally convinced me that I was not wrong, that the derogatory things I had heard about blacks were said out of some kind of hate, some horrible misconception about an entire race of people. I began to realize that maybe this wasn't the only thing in which my upbringing was mistaken. I gained new knowledge and broke through a barrier that I'd never even known existed. By getting to know Harold, in fact, in getting to know all my teammates, black and white, I reinforced many of my personal beliefs, the ones that ran so differently from Vic's and the other people in that small Missouri town. A seed had planted itself in my mind and was beginning to grow.

It was in my sophomore year that tragedy befell our team. Harold drowned. This charming, handsome, witty young man, so full of hope, was suddenly taken. Yet in my grief, I had another awakening, another attitude altered by new knowledge, new experience.

Harold was from Arkansas and was to be buried on his family plot. The entire team drove down from Missouri to attend the funeral and pay our respects. Arriving in a small town, with empty stomachs and sad hearts, my teammates and I entered a diner to at least fill the empty stomachs. As we filed in we were greeted with cold stares. The manager scowled and pointed to the black members of our team. "They can't eat here!" he pronounced. We were dumbfounded. We had heard of the civil rights movement, but we were untouched by it in that little college in Missouri. Suddenly we were shot straight between the eyes with the power and the hate that was pouring all over the South. We looked at each other, the shock quite evident in our eyes. Soundlessly, we all filed back out to the street. For if they refused one member of our team, they refused the entire team.

We went hungry to the funeral that day. And yet again, my beliefs were torn when I noticed that most of the people who attended the funeral that day were white. These were people who had watched Harold's basketball career; they had cheered him along and followed his progress. Were these the same people who would not allow us to eat in their diner?

Suddenly everything I had learned in childhood came under my scrutiny. I began to challenge different ideas, such as the ones that told me I wasn't okay, and I began to see what a small and closed world I had grown up in. College did more than fill my head with facts. It filled my heart with the hunger for wisdom. I had a long way to go, but I was beginning to learn. It was a confusing, but exciting process. Little did I know just how much my whole world would change in college.

One of the really great things about high school basketball was meeting other kids from other schools. Another great thing about high school basketball was the cheerleaders. I found the best of both worlds when I met Georgia. I met Georgia, a cheerleader from another school, when I was a senior in high school. We stayed in contact while I worked the oilfields, and when we ended up at the same college, we began dating. She appreciated my basketball prowess as much as I appreciated her cheerleading prowess. We were married when I was a college freshman.

I had grown up believing that I was stupid. One view of a belief is that it is a strong emotional feeling about something, almost always without real evidence. This was the case with me. I had no real evidence that I was stupid, it was just something I made up from the quality of interactions in the environment in which I had been raised. After all, back in second grade the teacher *proved* my stupidity to me and to the rest of the children. I'd gathered additional evidence over the years, not making the team, not being the champion, missing the final shot. It didn't matter that I had accomplished such incredible things: going to the state championship regionals, earning money to support the family, my work ethic… I focused only on those negative things that proved to me that I was stupid. Now that I was in college, I was determined that no one would discover my terrible secret. I worked hard, I studied hard, and I kept the secret of my stupidity intact. I was worried, though, that someday someone would figure out that I was faking it. My worst fear was realized one day when I was walking down the hall. I'd figured out earlier that the best way to keep people from finding out that I was really stupid was to carry a lot of books around. And if someone asked me a question, I would use the old teacher ploy, "Well, what do you think?" So here I was, toting an armful of textbooks, when I passed the "smart kid" clique. These were the brains of the school, the physicists and chemists and such. I knew who they were; I'm sure they had no clue who I was. But as I passed, I overheard a chance remark: "Those guys who major in P.E. are really stupid. All they will ever do is take P.E. courses and end up teaching history at some hick school." I was dumbfounded. I had been found out. Never mind that they didn't know who I was, never mind that their conversation was a generalization. I was convinced that they were speaking about me! Devastated, I thought, "Everyone must think I'm an idiot, 'cause I'm majoring in education so I can become a basketball coach. My secret is out." By the time I reached the end of the hallway, I had changed my major. I chose the toughest, most difficult subject I had studied to date. I became a biology major. I could hardly spell the word. But biology students were assumed to be very bright. I had to keep up the façade. The next day I let the word out that I had changed my major. Soon people were asking if I was going for pre-med. I would nod my head and smile and say, "Yeah, I'm thinking about it." Within two days of changing my major, everyone seemed to interact with me like I was a pre-med student. Suddenly I was in a new class of people. It was a heady feeling, once more being one of the 'elite,' as I had been when I played basketball. It was intoxicating for this boy who had been so abused, so put down. I was part of a special group, though I knew deep inside that I was faking it; there was no way I was smart enough to become a doctor. On the basis of an offhand remark by someone I didn't even know, I degraded myself, changed the course of my life, turned away from my goal, and became something I was not. But I sure worked hard to hide it. Again, decisions like this reach back to our childhood. Here is one more example where *circumstances* and *circumstances* alone determined how I felt about myself.

I was dumbstruck when my biology professor approached me and asked me to be his lab assistant. I couldn't imagine why anyone would choose me for such an important position, but obviously I had him fooled, too. I took the position anyway, and for two years I worked as his lab assistant. I needed money, so I had quit the basketball team after only one season, and went to work as an assistant manager of a movie theater. My work ethic came in very handy. In my sixty hours of work a week, I essentially ran the entire operation. I hired and fired, I ordered and tallied. While others were having fun, I was hard at work. All that and a full-time schedule at school. All that and a wife and baby. I ran this way for the next three years.

Georgia, our two sons, and I moved to Oklahoma to complete my last year of formal education. Carefully, we had saved what money we could. Georgia contributed her savings and worked outside the home during our last year of school.

I continued, as usual, to carry a full load of classes. I graduated in the summer of 1965 with a B+ grade average after four very challenging years. I received a Bachelor of Science degree in Education, having achieved a major in Biology with minors in English and Psychology.

THE AMERICAN DREAM

Somewhere in my realizations was the fact that I was not stupid. I may have been ignorant, but stupidity was not my problem. The spark was there, but I did not take the time to explore it, to look at the accomplishments I had made in the past four years. I was too busy surviving to appreciate what it meant. Besides, I needed to work. I wanted the American Dream.

From all my years of poverty, I knew I never wanted to be poor again. I wanted to have a life of abundance. I wanted to provide for my family all the things I had been denied. So while I enjoyed the contribution of student teaching for a semester, I felt I could not give my family the life I wished for them should I continue in the education field. So I went job hunting.

It wasn't easy finding a job outside of education. With a college degree, I found for the most part, that I seemed to be over-qualified. I was amazed. I had grown up thinking that an education, a college degree would be the key to the riches of America. I thought it would be easy, with that degree, to find a job; another notion that wasn't true. But nobody would hire me because I was too qualified, or in some cases, under-qualified for the job. I finally found work as a manager trainee for a small roofing company in Missouri. I was sent to Kansas City where I ran a roofing warehouse, loading and unloading roofing materials from boxcar to warehouse to truck.

Through it all, I wondered, what happened? Where is the pot of gold at the end of the college road? I continued to work at the warehouse, wondering if I should stay with the company and try to make it into something, or should I explore more of the world?

Having grown up in the country all my life, Kansas City was the biggest city in the world to me. I was amazed at the enormity of it all. I was positive that even New York could not be any bigger or grander than Kansas City. There was so much out there, surely there would be something better!

I talked and listened to the truck drivers as we loaded and unloaded cargo and I learned about the 'world out there' from their stories. I took a second job to pay off student loans. Again, I was assistant manager at a movie theater, for the same company I had worked with while I was in college. It was one of the finer theaters in Kansas City, so suddenly I was wearing a tuxedo for the first time. I smile when I think of the image: chambray shirt, jeans and boots by day, tux with cummerbund and patent leather shoes by night.

I was having new experiences all the time. I was twenty-three with a lovely wife of six years and two precious sons. I loved spending time with my boys. We'd play together. We joined YMCA Indian Guides, where we would go camping and canoeing, all in fellowship with other boys and their fathers. I taught them basketball and Duane later became a fine player in his own right. Randy was the scholar in the family.

When Randy was six or seven years old, he announced that he wanted to be an astronaut. President Kennedy had promised that America would put a man on the moon, and Randy wanted to be part of all that. Much to my later regret, I spent two years telling Randy that he should not want that. I felt he wouldn't be chosen, that perhaps he wasn't smart enough, or perhaps I could not afford to send him to the right schools. I squashed my son's vision because I was unable to expand my own vision. I thought I was protecting him. Randy eventually gave up his dream of being an astronaut, all because of my viewpoint.

This is one way we pass on beliefs from one generation to another. I'd had such a hard time growing up, I had attained so few of my own goals, that I was frightened for Randy. I wanted to protect him from the disappointments I had felt in my life. I just wanted to make sure his heart wasn't broken. My heart was in the right place, but my attitude was skewed, and Randy paid the price. A few years later, Randy was tested in school and was found to have an incredibly high I.Q. Was he smart enough to have become an astronaut? Undoubtedly. Even as a child, he was brilliant. He could solve a Rubik's Cube puzzle in a matter of seconds. Today, Randy is completing his education in computer science with a perfect 4.0-grade average. He is following his dream.

We can all remember some adult talking us out of some of our dreams. We've all had some parent or teacher tell us "you don't want to do that," or, "You can't do that." Most of us were told that we're not smart enough, not strong enough, not rich enough, not talented enough. We were prohibited by a lack of money, by religious restraints, by geographical barriers. We were like little robots being given various limiting beliefs that stay with us until death, unless we do some kind of intervention that explodes those notions that don't serve us well. History is full of limiting beliefs. The baseball player, Tris Speaker, said about Babe Ruth: "Ruth made a big mistake when he gave up pitching." Or Lord Calvin, President of the Royal Society in 1895, who said: "Heavier than air flying machines are impossible." Or Charles H. Duell, Director of the US Patent Office, who in 1899 said: "Everything that can be invented has been invented." He actually wanted to close down the patent office! Or, Robert Millikan, Nobel Prize winner in physics in 1923, who said: "There is no likelihood man can ever tap the power of the atom." Perhaps more personal, are two more interesting limiting beliefs expressed by two well know Americans. One, expressed by Grover Cleveland in 1905: "Sensible and responsible women do not want to vote", and one by Harry M. Warner in 1927 who uttered: "Who the hell wants to hear actors talk?" Beliefs bring challenges, and I was faced with a new one.

I remember well the first time I was taken out to dinner. I was in my early twenties. Having grown up in poverty, a fine restaurant was a completely foreign world. Nevertheless, I found myself in the company of others, sitting at a beautiful table with a linen tablecloth, gleaming silver and sparkling crystal. It was a fascinating world and I was delighted to see steak on the menu. I had heard of steak. I knew that it was the prime cut of beef, that the rich ate it all the time and boxers used it raw to take the swelling out of a black eye. I had even heard that people *ate* it raw! I wanted to taste it, to know what it was like.

The waiter came to our table. Of course, I was the first person he looked at when he asked to take our order. I sat up and made my order. "Steak, please," I said. "And how would you like that prepared, sir?" asked the waiter. The question hung in the air for a moment. I finally answered, "Why cooked, of course." This time the silence was thick. I felt my face redden, my heart thumped hard in my chest. Suddenly I was back in the second grade and the class was laughing at my stupidity and my ignorance. Once more my embarrassment pulled up those old emotions that I was a loser. I stammered and mumbled some response and soon the waiter moved on. As I heard my dinner companions order, I heard words like rare, and medium-rare and well done. It was a new language to me. And it proved to me once more that I would always be that stupid, shy, awkward kid that would never fit in.

The rest of the evening, I watched as my companions picked up salad forks, and handled the bread and butter. I observed the proper use of my napkin and where to put my wineglass. It was a forgiving environment and it was there that I began to learn social skills. From there I learned that a man in a tuxedo needs to behave a certain way that is not expected of him when he is in work clothes. I learned how to be a gentleman by mimicking those with whom I came in contact.

I knew those lessons were important, because I had seen all my life how people were judged by their appearances, their manners and their style of dress. I had learned that people were judged by their actions, by what they did or didn't do, by what they produced or didn't produce. My knowledge was not cognizant; rather it was an instinctual thought, an instinctual knowledge of survival that continued to serve me in my dual role.

PRIDE GOETH BEFORE THE FALL

I was still an assistant movie theater manager by night and a warehouse manager by day for a few more years. One day a close friend of mine from the theater business introduced me to a man who invited me to take a test to see if I was salesman material. As a lark, I did. I passed easily. It's most likely that anyone could have passed the test. I did, so I was offered a job as a commissioned life insurance salesman. Once again, my work ethic came into play. I found myself on the phone constantly. I became proficient at numbers and I learned how to speak with people. I became a master salesman. I led my office in sales in my first two years. Before the age of thirty, I gained life membership in the exclusive International Million-Dollar Round Table. This was a rare feat for a young man.

But instead of winning friends, I was losing friends. I was doing well, and I felt proud of my accomplishments. For the first time since I had played basketball, I felt I had accomplished a goal, that I was a hero, that I deserved the admiration of others. I had received sanctions from management for my outstanding sales volume, and I took it to heart. I was the king of sales and I expected everyone to treat me as such. While it's obvious now, at the time I didn't realize what was really happening. My arrogance was really taking a toll. I was influenced by my ego to the point that I was simply blinded. Arrogance had helped me make it through some rough times as a child, but now that arrogance took the form of aggression; I was on the attack. I reverted to the same style of aggression that I had employed as a basketball player. It was the only style I knew. I had a track record of arrogance and it helped me succeed. The pursuit of basketball influenced my behavior in the business world. The entire experience simply moved me one step closer to the emotional challenge that I would experience a few years later.

I was so full of myself that my marriage began to fall apart. I had worked long hours for many years and had little time for my family. With the added weight of my renewed arrogance, the result of management's recognition, the marriage simply could not withstand the additional pressure.

I was torn by my actions. The last thing I wanted to do was to cause my own family pain, yet it seemed absolutely unavoidable. In retrospect, what I now see was that I was absolutely unwilling to do whatever it took for my marriage and for fatherhood. Somehow I simply could not stand up and do the right thing. It seemed, after I had worked so hard for so many years, received my education, worked two jobs, when I finally stopped and looked around, I was unable and unwilling to continue with my family. I was able to justify my actions to myself, and I took whatever measures it required to get myself out. It was very painful for my wife, my sons and myself. I attempted to try to make things right with visitation privileges and child support, but obviously nothing could overcome this type of hurt or pain.

Suddenly, with my newfound freedom, I was even more confused and convoluted than I had been. Whatever vigor I had brought to my business – with the support of my family – vanished instantly. For the first time in my life, I was like a cork, bobbing on the ocean, no direction, no balance, and once more, in a great deal of pain. I felt guilty for abandoning my work habits, I felt guilty for abandoning my family, and I even felt guilty for not knowing where I was going.

I stumbled around like this for several years. I attempted to be a good father, yet deep down inside, I knew I was still a loser. On top of all my childhood shame, I now added lack of focus at work, inability to maintain the responsibility of being a husband, and certainly, an inability to meet the standards of being a good father. I was able to escape the direct responsibility of being a husband and father, but I could not escape the consequences of my actions.

Four years after my divorce, I again jumped into a marriage that was hasty and ill planned. During those four years, I had lost my frugal tendencies and began to spend money that I didn't have. As Rita Mae Brown so beautifully says, *"Insanity is doing the same thing over and over again, expecting a different result."* By her definition, I was certainly insane.

My marriage to Patty never had a chance. It began with infatuation and somehow turned into a love-hate relationship. Growing up, I was always afraid of the pretty girls. I rarely asked them out, and as I recall, the few times I did, I was rejected. Of course that fit my 'loser' pattern at the time and was very consistent with how I felt about myself. When I met Patty, she was the most beautiful woman I'd ever had the courage to ask out. I was shocked when she said yes. I read somewhere once that infatuation is making up for what one missed in an earlier life. I was, at first, very infatuated with Patty because I had missed out on dating, on going out with beautiful young women during my teens and twenties. She represented everything that I had never been able to have. She was a free spirit, very aggressive with her demands, self-centered, and a woman I found difficult to say no to in any regard.

Looking back, I can see now that she too, had a very low self-esteem. She too, had a great deal of trauma in her childhood. And just like me, she was a spendthrift who didn't mind living on the edge. While all evidence said, "Save yourselves," we both ignored all the warning signals and got married.

Our relationship was so volatile that we didn't even spend our wedding night together. The way we had both grown up, our backgrounds of standards, values and beliefs we had acquired from our environments along the way had both of us distrusting both men and women. So there we were, two people, infatuated, falling in love, scared, non-trusting, with terrible spending habits. Over our heads hung a cloud of impending doom. It seemed for the most part, that every day was a small war. There were times that we were able to nurture each other, but those times were rare. I can look back and see that those nurturing times occurred only when we both were feeling vulnerable and needy at the same time. Otherwise, we had no patience for each other's behaviors. Either way, we reverted to a childhood emotional state, one time being nurtured, one time being rejected. How we reacted to each other depended on the situation and the circumstance.

I found myself in a situation where my work habits were fragmented and poor, and my income uncertain. My relationship with Georgia was in tatters and my relationship with my sons drifted in and out of reality. My second marriage was in trouble before the wedding even took place. Little did I realize that I was already looking for a way out.

I can see now that my answer to pain was to try to escape it and find happiness somewhere else. I left home to find happiness when I was a teen. I left my wife and sons to find happiness. I shirked my responsibilities at my office to find happiness, and now it seemed if I could only leave and start over again, that everything would be just fine. I was to discover that it would first get much, much worse.

Both Patty and I had strong survival strategies, and neither one of us was shy in expressing our points of view. She, too, had been raised in a harsh environment. Neither of us really knew how to sit down and talk things out. Have you ever sat down with someone you care for, hoping to have a sincere conversation with the promise not to become angry, yet within a few minutes, there you are, one more time, arguing, and yelling at the top of your lungs. It was this way with Patty and me. We cared for each other a great deal, we wanted to be together, and it seemed the more time we spent together, the more it drove us apart. It certainly didn't help, given my background. Not only did I not trust women, I was extremely jealous in those days. Because I was so jealous, I became possessive. I don't know if I even had a healthy respect or regard for women back then. I had seen how my mother was treated. From time to time, I had argued with mother for marrying a man like Vic, who treated me so poorly. I brought all of my history to this relationship. I was to realize in later years that to be in a healthy, nurturing relationship with men or women, one

must be at peace or closure with one's parents. To move forward in relationships in a healthy way, to be at peace with what your parents did or
didn't do for you, is critical. It often requires acceptance and/or forgiveness, and I was not in touch with closure at the time.

Not having that closure definitely heightened the drama in this relationship. Looking back, Patty was clearly doing the best she could, as was
I. I realize that had I known what I know today, the relationship could have
been much more nurturing, much more constructive than it was.

I went in and out of illnesses, I overspent, and never had much money
left over. My relationship with my two sons was strained. No matter what
I did, no matter how hard I tried, it all seemed to get worse. I couldn't figure out why – if I worked so many hours – how come I never seem to get
out of debt? I couldn't seem to please anyone anymore, least of all myself.
I desperately wanted a change.

In an effort to start life all over again, I received an offer, still in insurance sales, from a good friend, Paul, in Houston. Patty and I moved there
in the late seventies. It excited me. Here was a chance to start fresh. I had
a great opportunity and was making much better income, compared to
my previous jobs. Houston was like a golden dream. I had been to New
York by now and had seen the vibrancy, the life, the energy that surged
through the canyon-like streets of Manhattan. I felt it again in Houston.
Texas, so huge and so alive, was captured in the lights of Houston. I felt
as if I was living the movie, *Giant*. I was one of the young lions and
Houston lay before me like the windy, golden veldt of Africa, ripe with
business opportunities.

For the first time in my life, I was making what I considered a great
income. But I still had no education in handling money. Pretty stupid
behavior considering my history. I had never learned how to make my
money work for me. I only knew it as a tool to acquire what I needed and
wanted. So I continued to squander my money on the things I thought
would make me cool, would help me be accepted. I'm sure I looked quite
foolish to others at this time, but I didn't think of that. I only thought of
having the trappings and the toys and the entertainment, everything I never
had growing up.

It wasn't long after Patty and I arrived in Houston that we separated. It
was a separation that would last several years until our divorce. During the
years of separation, our relationship was simply another version of what it

always had been. Time and time again, we would attempt to work things out. Time and time again, we would fall into disarray, for our outlooks remained unchanged. We would go in and out of our hate-love-hate relationship. There were moments of joy and bliss, but they were overcome by moments of anger, hurt, revenge, frustration, and great sadness. It was almost as if Patty and I were in the background while in the foreground, our past beliefs, opinions, and histories took center stage and battled for survival.

During part of this time, I was almost completely alienated from my sons who still lived in Missouri. I had few friends at work – not surprising, considering my arrogance. And my life, while it seemed I was living it moment to moment, was certainly anything but living in the present moment. My relationships with women in general were at an all-time low. I was stressed; my work ethic – the one that had taken me through college – had become practically nonexistent once again, and my debts had become overwhelming. I was involved in nothing but shirking responsibility in every aspect of my life.

By then, I lived in a one-room apartment. I had lost my family; I was facing another divorce, and my sons were unhappy with me. On one sultry Houston morning I stood, looking out the window at my beat-up old car. I had been unhappy for some time. I couldn't manage my relationships with women, I couldn't manage my relationships with my sons, I disliked my job. I may as well have been back in the country, broke and without anything, just like when I was growing up in the sticks. What else could possibly go wrong? I was about to find out!

CATHARSIS

That morning, the radio played a popular song by Peggy Lee that had the sad refrain, "…is that all there is?" I became unsettled. At first I ignored the feeling and went on to my appointments. But somewhere along the freeway, as I was driving to my next appointment, the feeling came back. This time it would not be ignored. I remember music was playing. Suddenly I was having what could be called an 'emotional setback', though that would be an understatement. I felt ill. Overwhelmed and losing control of my emotions, I pulled over to the shoulder, turned off the engine, then laid my head against the steering wheel and sobbed.

While all seemed lost in that moment, later in life I saw a quote that more accurately reflected what was going on that day:

All the books of the world full of thoughts and poems are nothing in comparison to a minute of sobbing, when feeling surges in waves, the soul feeds itself profoundly and finds itself.[3]

I cried for what seemed like a lifetime. In that moment, it all came crashing down around me – my children, my marriages, my job, my mother, my childhood, my life – it all became too much to bear. So I sat in my car on the shoulder of the freeway and cried and cried until I could cry no more. I didn't know what was wrong, I just knew I couldn't go on this way. I knew I needed help. I wiped my face dry, started the engine, and drove to the nearest bookstore where I began my journey to the future by buying a stack of self-help books.

I read and combed through every one of those books. I started attending any and all self-help seminars and workshops. Soon I was working even less than I had been, since I was spending the majority of my time in seminars and workshops. I went to every workshop I could find, looking for ways to ease my pain. Initially, I participated in meditation, transactional analysis, and group therapy. I even went to a psychiatrist for a time. I searched and searched to find a way to make it right, to cure me and make me a whole person, capable of love and free of emotional pain.

I continued to search. I unwittingly was becoming a student of communication, a student of relationships. It was all out of a need to survive. Though I didn't know it at the time; I was still just stumbling around, but it was a new direction for me. They were incredibly difficult years for me. It seemed it all got worse before it got better. I felt like my life was going nowhere, that I was on a treadmill running as fast as I could to nowhere.

One day, I stumbled into yet another seminar, just waiting for the magic to happen. As it hadn't yet, I did not hold out much hope that it would that night. But then the speaker said something about the quality of my own life being up to me. It was up to me to determine if the glass of life is half full or half empty. How I interpreted life was my decision, not my *circumstance*. It was all up to me, how I felt about myself and others. This was a giant breath of fresh air for me.

As simple as that sounds today, back then it was revolutionary to me. Feeling like a loser most of my life, as I had by being emotionally and physically abused, I never wittingly realized I was always at the effect of my *circumstance*. Oh, I knew superficially I didn't count unless I scored points for the team, or I sold the most, or I made the most money, had the nicest things. But, for the first time, I was able to see that I could be more than just the sum of my accomplishments. I really heard what that speaker said. Suddenly, in that instant, the direction of my life changed forever. I began to see that perhaps all things *were* possible for me. I started realizing that, while I could not change people around me or my past mistakes, I could alter how I related to them.

I realized that my 'inner-self' was separate from my *circumstances*. It was not the things happening to me that made me what I am, it was my reactions to them. I had always lived my life reacting to outside *circumstances*. I allowed the *circumstance* of the situation to define who and what I would be, and how I would act. I saw that I could either be a hostage of my *circumstances,* or I could just *have circumstances*. Now, for the first time, I realized that emotions associated with the label of 'loser' were more appropriately defined as 'victim,' a new label that was difficult to take on. However, seeing that I did have the power, if not the knowledge to separate my '*inner-self*' from my '*circumstances*' was truly exciting for me.

It was revolutionary. If someone said something unkind to me, I finally realized, I did not have to let their words intimidate me, nor did I have to be a victim about it. I did not have to succumb to the statement. It really was up to me. Sure, it was there and I might not be happy about it, but I did not have to react to it. I did not have to allow my energy to be drained away. For instance, if I don't like it when someone is late, I can be a victim, and blame the other person for how I feel, or I can chose to have the circumstance be unimportant and move on emotionally. I can refuse to be a victim of the *circumstance*. However, if I fail to move on emotionally, I have in essence combined two pieces of myself. I have combined who I am (my '*inner-self*') with what surrounds me (the *circumstances*), which creates a lot of mind chatter.

I was now able to look at my past and see why I could be a jealous person. It was just one more characteristic I had acquired from my environment growing up. Jealousy had cost me relationships, it cost me energy, it cost me time, and it even cost me my sanity on occasion. I realized that I had combined a multitude of things. I had collapsed my '*inner-self*' with a *circumstance* called jealousy. When I saw or imagined a certain thing, or felt a certain way, I *became* that *circumstance*, jealousy. I was finally able to see the difference between my '*inner-self*' and the feeling of jealousy. From time to time, I had exhibited jealous behavior. It was separate and distinct from whom I really was, my '*inner-self*.' Now I saw I had control over whether to go to that dysfunctional emotional place or not. It was very powerful. This knowledge was powerful, but it was also frightening, as the first step to any life altering journey can be.

I was still separated from Patty and my sons were still not in good relationship with me, yet everything looked different. While the marriage did fail, over time our relationship became one of respect and acceptance of each other.

Along the way, I found myself participating in many different disciplines of self-help. I consistently put myself into environments that challenged my personal growth in the area of personal responsibility, and eventually, I furthered my training in public speaking, starting with a Dale Carnegie course. As my role in public speaking grew, I found myself crossing the country for different organizations as my area of presentation became focused on communication and relationships. It was a topsy-turvy time, but there was always progress. It became clear to me that I was simply teaching what I had to learn, that I was actually engaged in a program of self-healing. One of the most frightening things I had to work on during this particular phase of my journey was my 'victim' mentality. It was, and is forever a deep-rooted and deep-seated piece of me, and even today I must be extremely vigilant to not regress in this area. I found that issue to be at the root of most all of my problems, that indeed, every problem I seemed to have somehow went back to this basic foundation that I had built as a child. As I sorted myself out over the years, I was able to regain my work ethic. I became intimate with what *self-responsibility* actually meant and I was able to start living my life from that principle in a consistent manner. I learned that my word meant something; in the final analysis, all that I had was my integrity and my honor.

I learned about communicating under the most stressful *circumstances*. I learned about listening to others' points of view without imposing my own. I was able to untangle my childhood and begin to see what really happened. I was able to start putting things in a proper order. I discovered I truly was in charge of myself emotionally, and I could have my *circumstances* work for me rather than against me. Rather than reacting to *circumstances*, I could be mindful and represent my '*inner-self*' which is where freedom lives, owning that which owns us.

I saw what my arrogance cost me. I saw what my past attitudes cost me. I realized how I had lost my first family, my second wife, and several business opportunities. There were many difficult times. I had to go deeper and deeper into myself for more and more truth. I discovered things about myself that not only saddened me, but often left me feeling hopeless. As I gave up many of my old patterns and acquired healthy new ones, I found the direction of my entire life changing. I changed careers several times during my self-exploration, as there were enormous opportunities presented to me. I was finally able to obtain what I had been chasing all those years: consistent respect as a person who was known to produce results, doing whatever it took within the boundaries of integrity. Even though I started organizing my life around these higher principles, I still found most interactions a real challenge. Every time my past standards were violated – in that split second – I had to choose either to go down the old path, where pain and suffering was always waiting, or a new way. This meant being willing to give up previous behavior patterns, as well as being very mindful of my ego. I think ego has us either being 'better than' other people or 'not as good' as other people. There's a demanding challenge in that split second to take the higher ground, and I was not always successful! There was a lot of pain in this growth and development. It was a lot like the Texas-two-step: two steps forward, and one step back, two steps forward, and one step back. What kept me engaged was the tremendous support of various people and my own willingness to have life be all that it could.

It took several years of research, and a real commitment to learn the lessons I had missed growing up, and to alter some of my past behavior patterns. I also discovered what had happened a few years earlier, when I had to pull off the highway sobbing. That day on the freeway, there was a particular song playing on the radio. I'm sure I'd heard it at other times, but that morning on the freeway I was feeling particularly vulnerable. That morning, the song threw me back, emotionally, in time to the Dairy Queen when I was sixteen. It was the night of the last game and I had taken the final shot and missed. We had lost the game. Though teammates kept telling me that everything would be okay, not to worry, I really felt bad. What the song had triggered on the freeway that morning was to open up a long, emotional corridor, or string, twenty-five years back into time. It was the same song that had been playing at the Dairy Queen after that particular game when I was feeling like a loser.

The incident at the Dairy Queen was simply added to long string of emotions that told me I was not okay. The song, in this instance, was the glue that held it all together. So here I was, driving my car, when the song triggered all the moments, in a linear fashion, of those countless times I had felt so lousy about myself. Back to the child who was stupid, back to the baseball fields where the other children laughed, back to being cut from teams, to missing the final shot. Given my vulnerable state, the song triggered in me memories of past failures. I was a loser as a kid growing up, I was a loser in basketball, I was a failure in marriage, I was a failure as a father. Clearly, the song was the reminder that triggered that barrage of emotions. This is how easily one can be thrown into emotional confusion and upset – over a song, a word, an odor, an image, or a thought.

But now I had new tools, a new way of seeing things, and new doors had been opened. During this time, with the massive changes I was making within my '*inner-self*', I was finally able to again engage in conversation with my sons. I invited them down one summer to be with me, so I could start being more responsible as a parent, to start correcting many of my past errors, and to build a new future. They were excited. They wanted to come for the entire summer. I found them summer jobs, bussing tables and sacking groceries to support them on their own self-responsibility path. The boys came to me with some apprehension, of course, but they weren't as scared as I was. I knew that I had years of unsaid things to say. I knew they had years of pain to address with me. It was uncharted territory, and it was the most confrontational thing I had yet faced. I doubt that a day had passed that I had not felt the pain of having abandoned my sons.

The first few days, my sons and I cautiously interacted. We were careful with what we said, what we asked. Conversation was forced as the three of us looked for a way to start what we all knew would be a challenging conversation. Finally, late one night, not long after they had arrived, Duane asked me if he could really talk to me. Could he really say things that were bothering him? He was asking if it was safe for him to be straight with me. In the previous days, I had tried different ways to encourage them to talk to me, to let them know it was safe. Though I assured him that it indeed was safe, I was totally unprepared for the direction the conversation took. I knew that the single biggest contribution I could make was to keep my mouth shut, and to listen from my heart. I knew I had to be fully present and available. It was probably the longest, hardest night I had ever gone through in my life. Duane talked for hours. Time after time after time, I wanted to interrupt. I wanted to change something he said, wanted to defend myself, to alter his perceptions. I wanted, in the final analysis, to look good, be right, even though I knew I had but one job that night, to listen to my son, to really hear and see how it had been for him, from his point of view.

Life without balance can be a challenge!

He started by talking about when he was five years old, about something I had promised to do and hadn't done, something that I didn't even remember. He went chronologically through his life, through the last ten years. It took hours and hours and it was all I could do to stay in the room. He reminded me of the time I had said I would come to the school play, and somehow I had been too busy. He reminded me of the time I was going to come and play baseball, and somehow I had something more important to do. He reminded of a time I was going to take him on a canoe trip, but I replaced that with my own concerns. He reminded me of the time I said I would practice basketball with him, to help him make the team, and how I was a no-show. He had years of pain over my leaving his mother, and he let me know about that. Of course, most of the things he said I knew were true, and a lot of the things he said – while they were not true for me – from his perspective, in his world and in his life, were his truth. I had never cried so many tears, nor had I ever been so touched by that much pain at one time. This far exceeded any pain I had felt as a child.

My son peeled back the years, and peeled back the layers of pain that he had gone through. As we purged our hearts and our souls, by early morning we started to come out on the other side. Obviously there was nothing I could do or say that would change any of that, all I could do was be there, to hear my son with all my heart, and ask him for forgiveness and acceptance, and, finally, commit to a new relationship. When that moment finally came, I was filled with self-loathing, pain, shame, guilt and a lingering question: Would I ever be able to make it up to this courageous young man? Through his eyes, I saw the pain I put his mother through, and I realized how badly I'd affected the lives of three people I loved dearly and how what I'd done would impact them the rest of their lives. It was probably at that moment that I realized what it really did mean to be '*self-responsible*' in the area of relationships and the tremendous cost we all paid as a result of my previous actions.

Finally, my son responded to my plea of forgiveness. He reached out and took me into his arms. He held me. We sobbed together for the longest time, holding each other for the first time that painful night. In my heart I committed to the integrity of our relationship with a new promise. Duane was generous in his forgiveness and his compassion. He had the heart and the eyes to see past me to the bigger future, and, he too saw a brighter future in our relationship, much more so than I could at that moment.

The rest of the day was a tangle of emotions. I would laugh, I would cry, I would be sad, I would be happy. I was bouncing off the walls. One moment I was elated that I had my son back, the next I would be devastated at the pain I caused. What also became clear was that his mother would probably never forgive me for the incredible pain that I had caused her. Over the years, I reached out to Georgia, to be in relationship. While it can be a bit awkward, we are able to talk about our sons and grandchildren, and for this I am grateful.

Late that evening, when I was still emotionally raw from the night before, my younger son, Randy asked for the same opportunity. With joy, I said yes. In my mind I thought I could handle this easily; after all, look what I had handled the night before. I thought it would be simple this time. I doubt that I have ever thought anything more wrong in my life.

Randy went even further back than Duane did. Randy went back to when he was three, and with an incredible mind for detail and organization, I was in for another long night. What had happened between Duane and me in no way prepared me for Randy's communication. Randy not only remembered things like missed baseball games and school plays, he remembered looks, little remarks I'd made, slights and zingers. And of course he seemed to remember every promise I had ever made and then did not keep. One of the things that left a cold place in my very being was when Randy reminded me that he'd wanted to be an astronaut, but I convinced him that he couldn't be.

He remembered all the grade cards that I hadn't even seen, that his mother had signed; he remembered the science projects that he so proudly brought home and that I never saw. He told me of daily conversations with his teachers, with his mother, with his friends, conversations that were important to him and I hadn't been there. At one point he had taken on the entire school, defying some mandatory activity that he thought was not right. He'd been suspended for his action, yet I was not there for him.

If I thought the first night with Duane was brutal, this night made me realize that Duane had been gentle. Not that Randy was being cruel, he was simply speaking from his heart. All he was doing was sharing with his father how it had been with him. This time with Randy again took most of the night, and again my job was to listen, to put myself in his shoes, to experience his pain, to see how it had been for him. It was the second hardest night of my life, and remains so today. Even so, Randy, too, was generous in his forgiveness and in his acceptance of me. He, too, committed to start fresh with me.

Even now, as I look back on those two evenings, I see the power of this incredible turning point in my life. It has changed *all* my relationships, not just my relationships with my sons. It woke me up to the fact that it is so easy to misinterpret, how easy it is for us to lay blame and shame and guilt on others as we go merrily about our business, doing what we want.

We seem to be a society that is more committed to what we want rather than what actually makes sense for all of us. I, of course, represented that point of view better than anybody I've ever met. I was fortunate that I was in a state of mind to be able to hear my sons. If I had not done work in the area of self-growth and *self-responsibility*, I am convinced that not only would I have not heard my sons, I would not have a quality relationship with them today. Without the years of work, without being willing to look at myself truthfully, without being willing to alter certain ways that I saw the world, I simply would not have been available to my sons. What I went through those two nights I would not wish on anyone, but by the same token, I would not ever give those nights away. My sons gave me a gift those nights that became a pivotal turning point that absolutely no one else on the planet was able to give me.

At one time I regarded gifts as something that gave me pleasure, something that I looked forward to receiving. Over time I realized that all of life is a gift, the good, the bad, the ugly – especially the ugly, for that is where the real gift lies. One of my commitments in life is to realize that everything that comes to me is on track, especially the situations I don't like, especially the circumstances I don't want to look at, that bring me to the edge. When I can see that everything brought to me is a gift, life is much more fulfilling than when I have the arrogance to pick and choose what gifts I will accept.

Having made good with my sons, we spent many summers together. We rafted and biked our way through the hot, steamy Texas days, and I watched proudly as my sons turned into young men.

REBIRTH

Over the years, I continued my speaking, traveling nationwide. In my travels, I learned that there were no accidents, no coincidences, that there was a reason for everything that had happened to me up until then and that there would be a reason for everything to come. I realized that all of life has meaning and messages, if I was willing to look for them.

I learned that life wasn't just about the good times. I found out that life is meant to have challenges, is meant to have ups and downs. How we interpret life is the key. It's easy to live the good times, when circumstances are consistent with your feelings. But, what about the challenges? What about when I felt stupid and unworthy? What about the failures of my marriages? What about the failures with my children, with money, with friendships? Those were times that counted, those were the times that, ultimately I learned were important. I wasn't stupid, I was just ignorant. Though I had missed the opportunities from time to time, I could still look back and learn from them. I could take those experiences and make corrections into the future.

One of the greatest joys to happen to me out of all the years of speaking was meeting Sue. I had seen Sue come into a meeting one time. I thought she was the most beautiful woman I had ever seen. From a distance, in one single instant, I fell in love. From time to time over the next two years, I would see her in and out of various seminars, yet I never spoke to her. She was married and one of the things I had come to appreciate fully was that I had standards, boundaries, integrity. So I watched from afar. Two years later, we met again. In our brief meeting, she informed me that she had given up on her marriage and was getting a divorce. Having been through two divorces, I could readily identify with the pain, and I knew how hard it was, especially since she had two small children.

As she separated from her husband and started divorce proceedings, I was able to spend time with her. Eventually the divorce was final. We continued to see each other. Two years later, we were married. Our union gave us a large blended family as we joined seven million other blended families in this country.

Sue and I had a lot in common. We'd both been raised in challenging environments; we had both experienced divorce, low times and high times. Sue was the mother of two very precious boys, Jerran and Andy, ages six and eight, who, ironically, were the same age my sons had been when I divorced their mother. It was an honor to me to have a second chance to help raise two young boys. It was an opportunity I had passed up before, and I had no intention of doing it again. I had left my two sons behind when I divorced Georgia. Sue's two boys stayed with her. I had a sense of what it might be like for her former husband, Bob. While he seemed to be much more attentive to his sons than I had been to mine when they were young, there was still a great deal of pain and grief.

Duane and Randy had graduated from high school by then, and they came to stay with us while they attended college. Spurred on by Duane's long-time dream of working with me, he, Randy and I started what was to be a ten-year work relationship and a great resolution of all the pain we'd endured. The boys, with Duane leading the way, started buying real estate, finding old houses, fixing them up and creating rental properties. Within six months they had built the business up so that they needed a crew and a couple of trucks. They were quite excited about their success. It became even more exciting when my mother's youngest son, my brother Paul (who was Duane's age) moved to Houston and joined the enterprise. Making a difference for people was great fun for them, as was working with me. So Duane's dream of working with his father was realized. It was a great treat having Duane's leadership and Randy's smarts working with us.

There were many good times with our new blended family. But there were rough times, too.

Sue and Bob had dissolved their tense marriage. When I came into her life, they were both still quite wounded and found in almost every occasion a reason to disagree. Usually, I would leave when they argued, thinking it was their problem to resolve and I pretended to have no interest in it. I felt helpless. It hurt to see Sue's and Bob's pain, but I felt there was nothing I could do about it.

But then I realized that it was not just Sue's suffering, it was the entire family's suffering. Jerran and Andy were suffering. Our marriage was suffering. The arguments affected us all. Sue and Bob were tired of it. They wanted to end the battles, they wanted the boys to know that both parents loved them, even though they may not be together anymore; yet they simply did not know how. So, with a commitment to the well being of their children, Sue and Bob agreed to allow me to mediate our first family meeting to clear the air, get on with life, and begin the healing process.

So here we were: Bob, Sue and I. It was not a happy congregation that day. You can imagine the tension in the room. We started the meeting with just the adults, but later brought in Jerran and Andy.

The technique I utilized was modeled on one I had learned in my six years of relationship studies. During this time, in the business world, I discovered a communication process that I ultimately re-designed and became proficient at installing in hundreds of offices. This was the same process that I modified and used in our first family meeting. There is an old saying: "We teach what we have to learn." That is what I had been doing for the last six years. I had been learning through my teaching how to communicate, how to make known my feelings without hurting others, how to resolve conflicts without destroying others, all the while healing myself.

Our first family meeting lasted more than three hours. It was a wild roller coaster ride, but when it was over we had broken down walls that had been erected strong and tall a long time ago. By the end of that meeting Sue and Bob were able to hug each other, they were able to look each other in the eye and say, "I love you," knowing that it was true. I was delighted to realize that this interaction did not elicit a jealousy response in me. Sue and Bob began to reconcile their differences, and Sue was able to begin to let go of the feelings of betrayal, abandonment, anger, sadness, and the pain of a failed marriage.

During the preceding years, Sue had done a great deal of personal growth work in her own right. Without her incredible commitment, without her huge heart, without her willingness to do whatever it took to bring her family into harmony, that first meeting would never have worked. Sue stepped far outside of what was comfortable for her. She took great risks that day and ventured where she had never been before. She was finally able to be straight and candid with Bob. She was finally able to resolve issues that had been unspoken, which had caused great anguish for her and for her family. This was possibly the first time that Sue could hear Bob's point of view.

Bob, too, had grown emotionally in those years, and possibly, for the first time, was able to hear past his hurt, his pain, his upset. Out of their incredible willingness to create a healthy environment for their sons, they were able to rise to the occasion and do some work that resulted in a great relationship that has lasted to this day. It was all the result of a family meeting that most people would say couldn't happen.

Two important rules resulted from that meeting. First, anyone could call a meeting at any time, subject to everybody's availability, and, second, no one could leave the meeting angry, that everyone must be in harmony before the meeting could end. We didn't deny the *possibility* that people might become irritated, hurt, or upset, and the point was to keep everyone feeling safe, to keep communicating. We felt that our group would have enough presence, enough strength to keep everyone there, help them feel empowered, and to have everyone feel loved and respected. Group meetings often provide an environment that one-on-one meetings don't: safety in exchanging points of view.

Over the years, many meetings were called. They were often difficult meetings. It was challenging sometimes to get everyone together. Sometimes people were feeling particularly vulnerable. It wasn't easy to resolve. Yet, ultimately what always produced the result was the incredible commitment we came to, as a family and as a group of human beings who saw the bigger picture than just how we were each feeling that day. This is what makes family meetings work. They are often challenging, often things are said that we would prefer not to address or to hear. Sometimes it seems it would be much easier not to relate these issues, it would be easier not to take responsibility and not take action. Yet, the results produced are far more satisfying than the results produced by default when one doesn't take them on.

The children called the majority of meetings. Soon, the children were *leading* most of them. It was there that I saw what a leadership role did for the boys. They were confident, they were strong. They often showed a maturity and responsibility that soon carried over into their school lives, their friendships and their dealings with the rest of the world. For the most part, they learned how to communicate with us responsibly, though not always, being that children are children. They would call on us to follow the rules, usually with love and affinity! We would coach them on occasion, and as leaders they were able to say things like, "Dad, you interrupted mom," or, "Mom, remember the rules." They learned how to ask for things, to negotiate for privileges. And they learned that 'no' really did mean 'no,' a concept that often seems to be foreign in our country today.

The boys were so proud to tell their friends of times when their mom and dad would get together after being divorced. They were proud to be able to say their parents were good friends, and this was often met with skepticism. The boys would relate how we always spent the Thanksgiving holidays together and sometimes for Christmas as well as their birthdays. They loved seeing the surprised faces and hearing the comments of their friends. Many of them had divorced parents or were also in a blended family. The boys almost always heard wishful remarks from their friends expressing they wish that they had that too, but they couldn't imagine that ever happening with their parents.

I continued to work on the process; giving the children the role of facilitator made the process work extremely well. I had taught the process in seminars. I had seen it work in offices. But when it came to families, the only advice I ever seemed to hear people give was, "You need to have a meeting with your family." No one ever seemed to teach people *how* to meet with the family, how to get past the talk and see real action. I decided then that the process that was working with my family could be taught to other families. I knew it could work. I had seen the results in my own home. Families needed to be taught how to resolve conflicts without resorting to punishments. *The Family Connection* concept was born. This process required going past the roar, as explained in this short tale from Africa:

A pride of lions is an incredible hunting machine. When lions get old, they are not banished from the pride. They have a very important role. As the younger lions stalk their prey, the old lions go to the far end of the veldt where they lie down and wait. The younger lions then pursue their prey toward him. The intended prey attempts to escape, but when they come close to the old lions, they let out a huge roar that confuses and frightens the creatures, who then turn tail and run in the opposite direction, into the jaws of the young pride, to their demise. Had they simply kept going past the roar, they would have been safe; the old lions would never have chased them. Instead they fear the roar and end up as a meal for the pride. In human relationships we are much the same. We fear the 'roar,' we fear what might happen should we open a difficult subject or a subject with which we are uncomfortable. If we would just go past the roar we would find that the danger, or consequence, is almost never what we anticipated. We would find that beyond the roar lie safety, nurturing, and empathy. We would find that the issue is not going to destroy us, if we only communicate and acknowledge what's in our heart.

In all my years observing people, I have learned something very important. Ours is a society that does not consistently acknowledge people. I see it constantly. When a person is given a compliment, most somehow deflect it, turn it away. For example: A woman is complimented on her dress. Her usual response is: "This old thing," or, "This isn't a great color on me." It seems that we cannot recognize the compliment for what it is, a gift of love and appreciation. We cannot seem to accept the acknowledgment of others because somehow it contradicts our low opinion of ourselves in the area in which we are being acknowledged. Since this cycle is so destructive, I included acknowledgements in *The Family Connection* process. I felt it was *vital* to acknowledge each other, to let each other know how we appreciate the efforts and the love we receive from them. Acknowledgment, simply stated, is a gift of grace, of love, and appreciation, from one *person* to another. Remember your manners! When someone gives you a gift, say thank you!

Our blended family grew up together, defying the odds. We gave each other the gift of commitment – to do whatever it takes. Forty percent of blended families don't make it. It takes about eight years for a family to truly assimilate, and just over half of the blended families ever get that far. Using the meetings and placing the commitment to family first, we grew stronger together, we found solace and support in each other. We found ourselves able to weather any storm that came our way; all because of the love and the power we gave each other and ourselves whenever we came together.

Meanwhile, I kept looking for an environment where I could teach what I had learned. I eventually ended up in the dental practice management field. I started my own company, and traveled the country, teaching management principles and communication techniques in offices and with large groups. At one point, I commissioned a study that analyzed the results of our management and communications processes. They interviewed a large sampling of individuals who had instituted our techniques. The group found that production and revenues had increased up to fifty percent. Offices were not working harder or more hours. They were just having more fun, with a lot less stress. This was a direct result of our communication process, the same one I had utilized for our family meetings.

Since work was more fun, it was more productive. The results astounded me. I knew the process worked; I'd seen it happen in my own home. But I didn't realize until then that the process could make life so much happier for so many more people, especially those who took their more positive attitudes home to their families.

I especially loved traveling to seminars in the summer. It was then that we could combine family and work, where the boys would join us on our speaking tours. I often spoke to large audiences, often thousands at a time. Andy and Jerran would be completely involved, running microphones up and down the aisles to audience members who had questions or who wanted to share stories. They absolutely loved selling tapes and products in the back of the seminar rooms. They were enthusiastic and had a great time.

At one large meeting, Jerran and Andy actually ran a question and answer session on stage, in front of hundreds of families. They spoke about how it was to be in a blended family, what it was like, going back and forth between homes, to have a stepdad and a stepmom. I was amazed by their insight, what they learned, what they saw. They were excited to talk about the family meetings and how the family meetings had made such a big difference in their lives. The boys were very candid. They shared some of the pain, some of the struggles. The family meetings were not always fun; they were not always easy to go through. Of course, what the family meetings were about was getting the end result, getting the family back in harmony and full affinity. Family meetings bring a deep and powerful commitment of love to each other. There are days and times in all relationships where, though we deeply love each other, in the moment we simply don't like each other. I can love my wife, Sue, dearly; yet there are times that I simply don't like her, and vice versa. The moment, the dislike, is a separate conversation from our love and our commitment. It's just the moment, when we are vulnerable, when we feel, whether true or not, that we have been offended. In that moment we may not care for that person. But it does not affect our love for them. That's a distinction, I think, that many people are not clear on. This lack of clarity can cause a great deal of suffering and pain.

Randy handled the logistics. He made hotel reservations, arranged for meeting rooms, ran all the audio and videotaping, and did an enormous amount of computer work.

Duane was a stage speaker. Duane would work with the staff people, teaching them how they could put away retirement funds, how to buy homes and cars, and how to shop interest rates. He took the mystery out of investment for a lot of people.

We were a true dream team, and we covered all the bases. Sue is incredibly talented at image consulting. She'd studied with Robert Pante', author and lecturer who enjoyed national fame in the field of personal and professional dress. Sue would work with individuals, showing them ways to present themselves in the best light possible. She taught them how to improve their dress, what colors and styles to wear, how to put a wardrobe together, and what makeup and hairstyles were most becoming. She had the ability to show people how to look and feel great about themselves. The six of us were more than simply a family, we were a true communion of spirits.

It was a true pleasure for our family to be together, traveling and working. We would venture to great cities such as New York, Los Angeles, Phoenix, San Francisco, and Chicago. We would stay an extra day or two, when the boys were out of school, and enjoy the museums, parks and the sights each city had to offer. It was truly one of the great times of my life, and I am sure, my family's.

How did it all turn out? Eventually, the boys and I went our separate ways after experiencing a great personal and work relationship. Paul moved on to Alaska to be near our mother, and our brother Terry. Today Duane works with a mutual friend in the building industry, while Randy is living in Denver with his family, working and completing his degree in computer science. Jerran graduated from NYU film school and is actively pursuing his career, while Andy graduated from college and owns several auto dealerships with his father.

Bob, Sue's former spouse and father of Jerran and Andy, married a lovely woman named Wendi. They extended the family further with Trevor and Mikey. Sue has also been involved in Trevor and Mikey's lives on a consistent basis. Sometimes they would stay with us when Bob and Wendi were out of town, and we would enjoy dinner out, or the zoo, movies, etc. As mentioned previously, our extended, blended family works so well, that for a number of years we had a tradition of bringing all the family together at Thanksgiving. It was an extension of demonstrating just how thankful we are to be in relationship. While today it isn't always easy with everyone grown and scattered, we all still get together at least once a year on the ski slopes of the Sierra.

These events sometimes remind me of another time long ago. I think back to my childhood, how I wanted to help the orphaned children. Now I realize that poor communication, poor relationships make orphans of us all. I have "begun to realize" my dream of showing children that they are loved and cared for and I realize that this is how I help them. I can spread the word to everyone. I can teach people the steps to communicate with each other, to resolve the conflicts, to bring peace and harmony to the world, one family at a time.

First, one has to learn to deal with the standards, values, feelings, and beliefs of each person involved, for ongoing peace and harmony. Without this, one is left with the barriers of communication, and that most likely is as good as it will ever become.

CHAPTER 7

Barriers To Communication

NOTIONS, STANDARDS, VALUES, FEELINGS AND BELIEFS

BELIEFS

The family unit can be a difficult dynamic. We bring into our new families the history of our parents and their parents, their notions, their behavior styles, their beliefs. Often we hand these down like they are jewels, a legacy of sorts. When I hear people say they can't alter something because "We've always done it this way," I cringe. What is the logic in doing something just because your mother did it because her mother did it because her mother did it. Get the picture? Sometimes our notions just don't make sense. But they are strong and real and because of our history, there are standards, guidelines that, when violated, cause emotional pain. But humans being humans, none of us have exactly the same background, therefore we each have different standards covering absolutely everything we view.

A notion, standard, or belief is how we feel about a subject, not always based in fact, but more often based on a feeling. Webster's says that, "A belief may suggest mental acceptance without directly implying certitude or certainty on the part of the believer." In other words, a belief could be a strong sense of certainty without an 'in-fact' basis for the belief. This is what seems to dominate people's conversations.

What is 'accurate' or who is 'right' about today's weather? I have heard people argue over the quality of a day weather-wise. I have heard people differ on just about any subject imagined. Most disagreements are no more than individual histories clashing against each other, each person vying to win the day. This results, of course, in the other person being invalidated, indeed, if not both people.

My friend, Cindy, recently told me a story about her neighborhood. She lives in a hundred-year-old house in a neighborhood where the average tree is a hundred and fifty years old. These trees have grown together, creating a canopy over the street that is stunning. Recently, my friend was sitting on her porch, enjoying the morning, when four houses down, a truck pulled up with 'tree surgeon' written on the side. Men got out of the truck, grabbed chainsaws and approached one of these ancient, beautiful trees. My friend, being partial to the trees, promptly approached the owner of the tree. "What's happened? Is the tree sick?" Cindy asked. "No," replied the woman, "It's perfectly healthy." Cindy was shocked and delved deeper, and her response was: "I can't wait to see the look on my neighbor's face when she sees this tree is gone." It seems that the neighbors were having a spat, and knowing how the neighbor was fond of the tree, this woman was willing to destroy the tree just to spite her neighbor. Cindy tried to reason with the woman, but to no avail. Before long, the majestic tree was nothing more than firewood.

This is a prime example of fulfilling the old saying, "Cut off the nose to spite the face." This woman was only interested in getting at her neighbor. She was in no way interested in listening to Cindy. She was in no way interested in resolving the existing conflict.

Our culture struggles with listening, because we tend to listen for something we agree with, or to find something to disagree with, thus forming the basis of the conversation, and indeed, sometimes the very formation of the relationship. In other words, within our conversations, our beliefs have us watching each other to find what we agree and disagree with. What we are actually doing is looking for people just like ourselves, people who have similar likes and dislikes, like golfers look for golfers. Aren't all clubs, groups, and associations based on this premise? Ask yourself this question the next time you are in a group of people: "How many times did I look at another human being and invalidate them without even saying a word?" How did you judge the way they acted, how they dress, how they look? And, what about their size, their weight, their color? How did you feel about what they were saying and their body language?

Recently, I was in an airport after a long day of travel, when I stood near the boarding gate, simply observing. My row had not been called. First class passengers were busy boarding when suddenly an attendant came down the walkway, upset because the plane wasn't ready. In the next ninety seconds, two managers and two attendants began arguing, keeping their voices low so as not to disturb the three hundred people, now on hold, waiting to board the plane. I was close enough to hear their animated discussion. The argument was centered entirely on how the plane should be boarded. These four representatives, who, according to their lapel pins, had been with the company a long time, were all disagreeing on the correct procedure for boarding the passengers. They were harried, stressed and running behind time. They had three hundred people watching every move they made. And, of course, they were trying to be consistent with the policies and procedures of their company. Finally, in the middle of all this upset, the ranking member of the group made a determination. Two people seemed happy, two people seemed unhappy, and the three hundred people were happy to finally be boarding the plane and not standing around while these four people sorted out their differences. What I saw was that no one was listening, opinions were clashing, and policies about taking care of people were in dispute, and the result was an untimely, unseemly demonstration of exactly what we are talking about here: ramifications that are a result of backgrounds in conflict.

Someone once sent the following story to me, author unknown. I would like to share it with you:

There was a little boy with a bad temper. His father gave him a bag of nails and told him that every time he lost his temper, to hammer a nail in the back fence. The first day the boy had driven thirty-seven nails into the fence. The second day the boy drove twenty-five nails into the fence. The third day, the boy drove fifteen nails into the fence. Day by day, it dwindled down, until the day came that the boy didn't lose his temper at all, therefore did not drive any nails into the fence.

He told his father about it and his father suggested that the boy now pull out a nail for each day that he was able to hold his temper. The days passed and the young boy was finally able to tell his father that all the nails had been pulled from the fence. The father took his son by the hand and led him to the fence. He said, "You have done well, my son, but look at the holes in the fence. The fence will never be the same. When you say things in anger, they leave a scar just like this one. It won't matter how many times you are sorry, the wound is still there.

The father went on to say, "A verbal wound is as bad as a physical one. Friends are a rare jewel indeed. They make you smile and encourage you to succeed. They lend an ear, they share a word of praise, and they always want to open their hearts to us. One way to show your friends how much you care is by not getting angry."

How much patience do you have, especially if you're harried? Think about it. Do your children forget their chores? Does your husband squeeze the toothpaste tube from the middle? Who handles the money in your household? How is discipline dealt with?

Suppose, while you were growing up you had a series of chores to do. You learned that your brothers took out the trash and mowed the lawn, while you and your sisters were assigned the duties of kitchen and laundry. Now suppose your husband was raised in a home where the boys had few duties – mom took out the trash and a gardener who came to the house once a week did the yard work. So now, we have a wife who believes that her husband should take out the trash, and a husband who has never considered it his job. She gets frustrated whenever she has to remind him. He gets tired of her nagging. Soon, the trash may as well be a nuclear dump for all the trouble it has caused in the home.

But it's not the trash itself that is important. What is happening is that the couple has different viewpoints about the trash. So they fight and bicker, never getting to the real problem – belief systems. They have different backgrounds, different ideas, different convictions. They accuse each other of being the problem, but, in fact, they are not the problem; they *have* a problem between them: different viewpoints, standards, values, feelings and beliefs regarding a simple issue: trash!

When Sue and I were first married, initially we had a difficult time adjusting to the way I sometimes came home from work. Growing up in a large family, I often had to shout simply to be heard, a posture I developed out of my history. So when I came home at the end of the day, I might shout, "I'm home! Where is everybody!" Now, in Sue's childhood home, shouting was reserved for only those times when her father was angry. Shouting in her world meant that there was trouble. So her response to my shouted greeting was one of automatic fear, without thought, all instant and automatic. She was afraid that, since she was not standing at the door with my pipe and slippers in hand, I was angry, when all I was doing was greeting my family in the only way I knew how. Quite a few tears were shed before we would know how to come to a compromise and have an understanding on this issue. Simply put, I was careful to not raise my voice needlessly, and, if per chance I did, she was mindful that it in no way represented the experiences from her formative years.

Unlocking the barriers to communication is essential to being happy

With our alarming divorce rate and the huge number of single-parent and blended families, it could be said that our family cul-ture is at a crisis. I think our society has forgotten that, while marriages may not last, parenthood is forever. I think that we are seeing the consequences of society not realizing that about our children. One of the reasons blended families don't succeed is when two people have left their former mates and formed a new union, in actuality they carry the same attitudes, beliefs, and rules they've always had into the new marriage. Often, they seem to replace their former mate with one who has a different personality, but a similar history, a history that made the first union so objectionable. They may look different, they may dress differently, but the belief system is the same, or very similar. So when the rubber hits the road, in at least forty percent of the cases, nothing has really changed. The result is often another divorce.

This is a story I have heard over the years, which makes a great point:

One glorious Easter Sunday a couple had invited their friends and fam-ily to a special holiday feast. A beautiful whole ham was the centerpiece of the meal. As the husband helped his wife prepare the meal, he noticed that she cut the ends of the ham before she placed it in the pan. Curious, he asked her why, what does it do for the ham? She told him she really wasn't sure, she'd just seen here mama prepare ham that way, so she did the same. The wife suggested to her husband that he ask his mother-in-law. The guests all arrived, and soon they were gathered around a table that was groaning under the weight of the fabulous feast. In the center there sat the savory ham, baked to perfection. As he helped his mother-in-law to her seat, he asked, "Tell me, why do you cut off the ends of the ham?" She replied, "I'm really not sure. My mama had always done it, so I have done the same." So he turned to the elderly grandmother and asked, "Why do you cut off the ends of the ham?" "Well, dear," she said with a smile, "I never seemed to have a pan big enough to hold the ham. I had to cut the ends off to get the ham in the pan."

This delightful story shows plainly, the way some patterns and beliefs are handed down from one generation to the next. Someone cuts the end of the ham off for one reason, and others begin emulating the action, believing that it's the way ham is prepared.

I know of a company, that, when they examined their budget, found that one hundred thousand dollars a year was being spent on masking tape. When an event was held, the personnel would tape down virtually everything on the stage, from chairs and carpet, to the microphone cords, to the chalkboards and flip charts. The reason for this action was that the logistics manual said so. Someone in the company finally questioned the need for all this taping. After all, the stage equipment was quite sturdy enough. Well, an old timer in the business came forward and told how, in the early days they used portable chalkboards. You know the kind, with little shaky wheels and a wobbly structure. The setup crew would tape those wobbly chalkboards to the floor and reinforce the legs with tape so the speaker could concentrate on the presentation and not have to worry about the board skittering away from them. It was at this very time that the logistics manual was being written for the company. This procedure became a policy, a belief if you will, simply because that's they way they did it in the old days. Here was the company, throwing away one hundred thousand dollars a year on masking tape that was not even necessary, simply because fixing poor equipment with masking tape became a tradition that eventually was put into writing.

That is the nature of our attitudes and patterns. Most of the things we turn into beliefs are formed that way. We do something a certain way and say it's part of our personality. Most of us don't have a clue as to why we do the things we do. This is where difference of opinion comes in. It is here that we find people becoming very defensive of how they think and feel.

Once when I spoke, I conducted an experiment. I was speaking along, when I stopped and told a joke about noses. The people who were okay with their noses thought the joke very funny and laughed out loud. But I could see in the audience several faces that weren't laughing. I saw people who had issues with their noses. Maybe they thought they needed a nose job. Maybe they had gotten a bad nose job. Maybe they had big noses. Whatever it was, my joke offended them. From that point on, those people were no longer involved in the seminar. It was as if they had shut the door in my face. I could see in their expressions that they were telling me, "I was relating with you, I was enjoying hearing what you had to say. Then you blew it with that stupid nose joke." The only way I could affect someone is if I violated how they already felt about their own nose.

This is one reason why there is so much drama and trauma in relationships. People come together, and they bring with them different backgrounds and histories. If the husband is a big spender and the wife was raised to count every dime, then there will be problems. Someone is violating someone else's standards. The same goes for raising children. If the parents are diametrically opposed in their child-rearing beliefs, they will pass each style off to their children, and there will be fallout.

Many notions, like the ham story, are handed down from generation to generation, like family jewels and the rest are learned from your childhood environment. Many make sense: pay your bills on time, stop at red lights, come in out of the rain. Most of the things we believe in are mundane and common; we pretty much all agree on them and work within them. Then there are those notions that are unique only to ourselves.

There are individual patterns, cultural attitudes, and global notions. So it goes. One global notion that has proved false, but used to be passed around a lot was the idea that women were poor drivers. But statistics have proven that to be false. Statistically, women are much better drivers than men, but do all men believe that?

HOW ATTITUDES ARE FORMED

Once upon a time, a man whose axe was missing,
Suspected his neighbor's son.
The boy walked like a thief, looked like a thief and spoke like a thief.
But the man found his axe while he was working in the field.
And the next time he saw the neighbor's son,
The boy walked, looked and spoke like any other child.
—FROM TAO-JONES AVERAGES, *Bennett W. Goodspeed*

HOW BELIEFS ARE FORMED

Here are five categories that tend to affect and form our attitudes and how we believe: things that have happened, our surroundings, what we know, our past and future expectations.

Things that have happened. A woman I was working with once told me a story how she always, without exception, paid her rent early. As I asked her questions, her reasons came tumbling out. As a girl, she had seen her family evicted, because the rent was always late. This dramatic event in her young life fostered an attitude. She believed that if the rent was always paid on time, even early, she would never have to relive that horrible event. This piece of history will always shape her future when it comes to housing expenses.

Our surroundings. What kind of home did you grow up in? Was it a place of fear or a place of joy? Were you encouraged or discouraged? Was there punishment or consequences? The child who grows up with a lot of harsh rules will take those rules into adulthood. This all happens starting at birth. By the first year of life an infant will have learned about trust. In a loving environment, the infant will learn that her needs will be met whenever she cries. The consistent and loving treatment she receives will stay with her through her entire life. The infant whose care is inconsistent, who is allowed to cry without being cared for, will find that her needs will not necessarily be met and that she cannot trust those around her for support and care. These feelings of trust or mistrust are ingrained solidly into our minds in that first year!

What we know. These are the things we know to be true (whether or not they are fact or fiction). We know that the sky is blue. We know that there is day and night. And we know that smoking causes cancer. We also know that children should be seen and not heard, that we must treat strangers with more courtesy than we do our family members, that a lady never gets her name in the paper, that a college education is wasted on a female, that big boys don't cry, and that a broken mirror means seven years of bad luck.

There was once a time when everyone thought the world was flat. They believed that if you were to sail too far out in the ocean, you would fall off the edge into a great abyss. Some cultures still believe this. But we now *know* that the world is just as round as the sun the moon and the stars.

Other notions include the "big-boys-don't-cry" belief, the "good-girls-don't-talk-back" belief, and my all time favorite, the "children-should-be-seen-and-not-heard" belief. It is these conditions we use to set up the standards for the family and for ourselves.

Our past. Suppose every time you called a friend to invite him to dinner he refused, saying he had another commitment. Soon you would quit inviting him, right? Suppose, when you were a child you stuck your finger in a light socket. You got quite a shock, didn't you? And you learned never to do it again. When we see the results of our actions, hopefully we learn from them. Past results affect us strongly.

Future expectations. When I was finishing college, I began daydreaming about how businesses would be chasing me down, offering me outrageous salaries and fabulous perks. I had heard that a college degree would take me places, would give me a future that was guaranteed safe and prosperous. Of course that all changed when I entered the work force with my degree in my hot little hand. I found that there were many jobs that, even with a college degree, I did not qualify for. Even worse, most of the jobs I interviewed for showed that I was overqualified. I had the college degree, where was the future?

Anticipated attitudes and beliefs are those that we just know, if we do things a certain way, we will get what we are looking for. If we lose ten pounds before vacation, we'll have a lot more fun.

Here we are with all these perceptions. Some work, some don't. Now what?

ALTERING ATTITUDES

"When I was a boy scout we played a game when new scouts joined the troop. We lined up chairs in a pattern, creating an obstacle course through which the new scouts – blindfolded – were supposed to maneuver. The scoutmaster gave them a few moments to study the pattern before the adventure began. But as soon as the victims were blindfolded, the rest of us quietly removed the chairs. I think life is like this game. Perhaps we spend our lives avoiding obstacles we have created for ourselves, which, in reality, exist only in our minds. We are afraid to apply for that job, take violin lessons, learn a foreign language, call an old friend, write our congressman, whatever it is that we'd really like to do but don't, because of the perceived obstacles. Don't avoid any chairs until you run smack into one. If you do, at least you'll have a place to sit down."

—Pierce Vincent Eckhart

We usually do not alter our perceptions, especially if we feel strongly about them, unless they have cost us emotionally. For example: I grew up not trusting women. Remember, when I was a baby my mother worked long hours. An uncaring aunt tended me. Take that situation, add to that my mother marrying a man who abused me. How could I really trust her? Remember this all happened without any planning or thought on my part. It all took place automatically. Not having my needs met as an infant, I formed an opinion that women could not be trusted. Now as an adult, that opinion manifested as jealousy. The funny thing about perceptions – they never go away just because we wake up one morning and say 'go away.' There is work in altering negative perceptions, or how we believe:

- *Embrace the Attitude.* Acknowledge it as yours. Yep, I'm jealous, that's the truth. This can be embarrassing, and that is where you have to start!

- *Be resolved to altering the notion.* You can't be just mildly interested. You have to make it a matter of life and death. Like running out of air under water, you move as fast as you can to the surface. After all, it's a matter of life or death, emotionally speaking. Altering your negative perceptions or beliefs requires that quality of commitment.

- *Get support.* Surround yourself with people who will support you, who will help you catch yourself before you revert to your previous behavior.

What happens eventually is that you catch yourself. You notice the price you pay for your actions, or rather, reactions. You see how invalidating that way is. We only give away what we have. If I don't handle jealousy within me, I will be jealous of you, if I don't respect myself, how can I respect you? You need to love yourself in order to love others.

Altering a negative belief requires a strong commitment as well as strong support, because it never really goes away. What it comes down to is, are you going to manage it, or is it going to manage you? I manage jealousy now. Now I rarely experience the emotion of jealousy. It's still alive and well, it didn't go anywhere. It's just that now I have the tools to keep it under control. I have the ability to embrace that emotion, to own it and make it mine if circumstances thrust me into a situation where, in the old days, I would have normally become jealous.

Again, it's not the *circumstance* itself that creates the problem, it's our *reaction* to the *circumstances* that lead all the way back to a childhood emotional state. All the self-help books and tapes in the world will not help alter us until we are willing to do whatever it takes to alter the way we react to those unbearable *circumstances* that routinely occur in our lives.

WHAT ARE YOUR ATTITUDES?

What are some of your self-limiting patterns? Take some time to answer the following questions. Make up your own list. Write them down.

1) I don't like being: overweight, unpleasant, old, inflexible,…
2) I'm short of: education, time, energy, talent, willpower,…
3) I find it a challenge to: meet new people,
     earn enough income, exercise,…
4) I am unable to: dance, save money, fall in love,
     stay on a budget, lose weight…

As you examine the list you have made, ask yourself, "How can I alter that attitude, pattern, or belief?" Now write an answer that shows your negative attitudes in a positive light.

1) I can be: attractive, pleasant, flexible, young at heart,…
2) I can overcome challenges such as: education, ,
     energy, talent willpower,…
3) If I want, I am able to: cook, embroider, take pictures,
     overcome my past,…
4) If I want, I can: save money, fall in love, lose weight,…

To alter limiting behaviors, you will need to alter your perceptions of the situation. Using powerful statements is a beginning that helps to show you that different perception. Powerful statements can include:

● It's all a matter of perception. There are no failures, there are only results.

- I *always* have a choice.

- There is always a way, if I am willing to do whatever it takes.

- People love me, they just have different ways of expressing their love (This statement can be applied to virtually every person we run across in our daily lives. Even the fellow in the next car who is shaking his fist at you in traffic is expressing his love. It may seem angry and impatient, but at that moment, in that space in time, he is showing you as much love as he can express; as much as he has available.).

I am often reminded of a saying by my friend, author and lecturer, W Mitchell: "It's not what happens to you, it's what you do about it," and, in fact, that is the name of his book. This, from a man who is paralyzed from the waist down, and has scar tissue covering 75 percent of his body as the result of a motor vehicle accident and fire. He is right. Mitchell is an incredible inspiration to all that know him or who have been privileged to hear him speak.

To blame our poor attitude, our inability to love and trust, our self-absorption on our circumstances or our parents is a cop out. Sure, your life may not have been great when you were a child. That is no excuse to whine about your lot in life. As long as we come to each day with a new and fresh attitude toward our difficulties we can overcome them and use them as a stepping stone for continued growth. If we use that as an excuse, we do not grow in self-responsibility. Instead, we stagnate like a pond that has no inlet. Fresh water cannot make its way in to clean the pond. It becomes rank and slimy. This is what happens to our lives. We wallow in self-pity and blame others for our misfortunes; our souls become rank and slimy. Just like dialing a phone number, you can dial and dial all day, but if you're off by one digit, you will never get the call through. We make up standards out of our history.

STANDARDS

Your more important attitudes – the ones you are attached to emotion-ally – can also be called your standards, guidelines, or rules. They usually have us doing whatever we can do to avoid emotional punishment or pain as we know it. This generally means the opposite of this is some type of joy or satisfaction. What is one person's pain can be someone else's joy. We see a drug addict, flying high on heroin and we imagine that they are in enormous pain. They, on the other hand, would have us believe that they are feeling a great deal of pleasure. Again, it's all a matter of interpretation. Is the glass half-full or half-empty? It is based on how one interpreted life growing up, particularly, as psychologists tell us, before and by the age of eight or nine. Our past history forms our perception, and standards come out of those key perceptions. When your standard is violated, or you *perceive* that your standard is being violated (which is more likely), you may become irritated, upset, or angry.

For instance, suppose you have an important meeting at five o'clock. Your spouse has the car, but promised to get it to you in plenty of time. Well, things happen and your spouse shows up late. If you are a person who believes in being on time, this can be an incredibly upsetting incident. Your "On Time" standard has been violated.

On the other hand, you squint through your new Varilux bifocals in the direction of someone across the room, attempting to read a nametag. Soon you notice that their behavior toward you is cool, almost rude. You ask, "Is there a problem?" They respond, "You were really giving me a nasty look back there. I'm offended." You unknowingly violated their standard, but you will still be blamed. Perhaps your expression reminded them of the time their father "gave them the look." Whatever it is, the result is always the same: a problem.

Some standards, when broken, involve a high degree of pain, while other standards, when violated, cause minimal stress. Remember how Sue and I had to work through yelling. In my childhood home, yelling meant being heard. In Sue's home, yelling meant someone was going to be punished. Once we were able to recognize each other's perceptions, we were able to alter our behaviors and responses.

At one seminar, a participant suggested that he did not agree with what I said regarding rules, and said, "I have no rules, as I am always 'open'." I answered by asking him, "Okay, would you loan me ten thousand dollars?" He responded, "No way!" "Well then," I said, "you must have standards and rules about not lending money!" Everything we do is organized around our beliefs and attitudes and from them fall the standards, guidelines, and rules. In *everything* we do.

One way to reduce the disagreements in your environment is to learn more about your loved one's standards. Find out what their feelings are, and be mindful of them. Life was much easier when I learned Sue's rule about yelling. There was so much less disagreement and discontent, and all I had to do was keep my voice down! For me it was an easy one to alter. I just had to be mindful.

We learn a lot about people's attitudes and standards if we listen carefully to what they say. Ask a child about their teacher. You will hear things like, 'she's nice, she reads to us,' or 'she's mean. I wanted to finger paint, but she made me do math.' Those clues tell us a great deal about the child's notions. The child who says she is nice, she reads to the class, is a child who values reading, who sees time spent in this activity as fun. The child who is upset because she had to do math may be telling you that her boundaries are not well established and her teacher is violating the rule that the child can do what she wants. It's by these innocuous conversations and simple interactions that we find out what the standards are for others.

If you were slapped every time you reached across the table, soon you would not reach across the table. Just as we work to follow society's rules, we also follow the ones we ourselves have set up. We establish for ourselves a covenant of behavior, and we expect others to live by the same covenant. When they don't, we become stressed.

STRESS

When we perceive that our standards or rules have been broken, we become stressed. Think about it. The only time we become disagreeable, get angry, get stressed out is when someone has done or said something that offends our set of standards, or our perceptions. We try to justify our responses by blaming others. We do it all the time! We get impatient on the freeway when a car pulls in front of us. We think our needs are more important than others' needs, so we huff and sigh and wiggle while we wait in line for stamps at the post office. We yell at our children when they forget to pick up their clothes. We pout and sulk when our spouse goes out with friends instead of spending the evening at home, never mind that we told them we were okay with their plans, they were supposed to read our mind, and know that we wanted them at home.

All of these problems, these violations are the result of not having reconciled the issues of our childhood. As we grow up, our environment shapes us, and most of the standards, values, beliefs, and attitudes we bring into our relationships have no basis in fact. It's just all the junk we bring along in our kit bags that prevents us from having harmony in our homes. We justify our behavior, calling it our personality. But we are not just the sum of our experiences. We all have different personalities. There are strong-willed people and compliant people. There are optimistic and pessimistic people. There are extroverts and introverts. It is the event – *as experienced by the individual* – which forms the basis for the standards we make up.

Our reactions to the stresses we create from our history can be altered. We cannot change the personality we were born with, but we can alter the reactions we have. The only way to find harmony, to create a home that is truly loving, is to alter those attitudes and change the rules if they are not consistent with what you say you want. We need to challenge ourselves to let go of the fear, let go of the hurt. All those archaic ways of living need to be swept away with new knowledge, new understanding and a renewed commitment to family, and relationship.

All pain and suffering for each of us lives either in the past (if only I had…) or in the future (next time I will…). When people are in the present, they are not really in touch with their emotional pain. Emotional pain lives either in the past or in the future. Of course, whenever we hear input from others, whether it is constructive criticism or we interpret it another way, this is simply an example of us reverting back to our past or projecting into the future. Then we do what we predictably do, whatever that is, whenever we interpret another's interactions with us as criticism.

CRITICISM

You have finally done it! You worked hard, exercised, watched your diet and avoided falling into all the old eating traps. You finally shed that weight that was raising your blood pressure, causing back pain, and getting in the way of all the things you love to do. You're doing great! You feel energetic and revived and you want to stay that way.

The holidays are here and the family gathers together. There's turkey and dressing, potatoes sweet and mashed, veggies, cranberry sauce and gravy, and pies. It's an awesome feast and you enjoy it thoroughly, because you know now how not to overeat. Soon your mother looks down the table, spies your empty plate and says, "Eat some more, Ellen. You look like a scarecrow." This out of the same mouth that said, "Getting a little broad across the beam, aren't you?"

You have a choice here. You can take this criticism as evil and malicious, and by doing so, create World War III at the dinner table. Or you can detach yourself from the comment, distance yourself from the remark, and realize that this is your mother and she is only looking out for you, doing the best she can to help; even if her words sting. It really all rests in how you interpret another's remarks. You always have a choice, the cup of life is half full or half empty: it is always your choice. You can be generous with your point of view, or you can withhold from life.

Of course, the answer to all this is to detach, distance and not take things personally, though I know just how hard that is. I knew a nurse one time that worked in an adolescent psychiatric hospital with children who had substance abuse and molestation issues. They were severely troubled young people and often their ability to accept any type of feedback was nonexistent. Every day, she would hear the teens bicker. They would then tell her how so-and-so told them they were a such-and-such. She would give them a small science lesson: "Have you ever seen a duck floating around in the water?" she'd ask. "They splash and dive and swim in any kind of weather. Yet, the water does not soak through their feathers. The feathers stay perfectly dry, because the water just rolls off." Then she'd smile and say, "Be a duck." When the teens listened and took this perspective, they immediately calmed down, laughed a little and said, "Yeah, be a duck." Then they would walk off down the hall repeating, "Quack, quack, I'm a duck. Quack, quack." She said it didn't work all the time, but it did work more often than not. Humor is an incredible stress reducer. It would be great if we all laughed at our 'stuff' more. Remember: It takes something like 37 face muscles to frown, and about 14 to smile – stay young, smile a lot!

There are opportunities every day to criticize others. At home, at work, in school, during sports practice, there are a thousand little things we could pick on each other about. I don't know if there is such a thing as constructive criticism, considering how sensitive most people seem to be about feedback. It rarely, if ever improves a situation, and most often makes it much, much worse. It all depends on the listener's interpretation. From rolling eyes to violent rage, you may elicit a response that, to you, is not warranted. It all depends on how attached to the rule the target of your criticism is (the behavior, not the person).

Criticism has been around a long time. In a note criticizing a city's rush hour traffic, Thomas Jefferson said in 1790, ." . .we could go no more than three miles an hour." We criticize because someone is not doing something the way we think it should be done, and we take offense to criticism because someone else is telling us our belief is wrong.

Feedback is different than criticism in that it is supportive and informative. It takes time to master. And it has to be requested. An athlete implicitly consents to feedback when he joins a team. A student implicitly consents to feedback when she goes to school. In virtually any other case, you have no right to 'tell it like it is,' unless you have been invited to express your point of view.

There are a couple of ways to handle 'constructive criticism.' When I am being criticized, I start asking questions. If somebody tells me I am taking too long on a project, I might ask, "What is your timeline?" or "What does 'too long' mean?" If someone tells me, "You ought to take time off. You're working too hard." My response might be, "what do mean when you say, 'too hard'?" I would be looking for more information in order to deal with the concern, not something I might make up. So often, we launch the rocket without gathering adequate information, or we launch the rocket on some misinterpretation we have. Two people could be standing together and receive the same information, but how each responds to it depends on the perceptions of the individual, or their history.

When giving feedback, be positive. "You're really working hard, here, and there's lots of room for mistakes, yet you've made so few!" You don't want to beat the person up about it, and you don't want to go on endlessly about the problem or the concern. Make constructive suggestions on how to get the job done, such as, "Call Jim for that information." Be clear in what is expected, and give them a timeline.

The tone of your voice is important. Your facial expression is important. Your expressions and the tone of your voice convey much more of the message than the words themselves. Body language is universal and is easily interpreted by all humans. And that is what they will react to. When communicating, the message is delivered a certain way. It is said that words are only seven percent of the communication; thirty-eight percent of the message is delivered with the tone of voice, and the remaining fifty-five percent of the message is delivered with body language. There's a lot of unspoken comment going on in the course of a conversation. While only seven percent of a person's total communication comes from words, language is critical to how one interprets, how one feels about one's self and merely changing one word to another can sometimes reduce stress and enhance fun.

WORDS

Words, we know, are critical, but when we really tease them apart and analyze them, we can see how words can bring joy or suffering. If it is true we are what we eat, it is perhaps true that we are what we speak, both emotionally and physically. We can literally talk ourselves into being ill. We can literally talk ourselves into being losers.

If I close my eyes and say, "What is wrong with me?" my brain will automatically start listing all the things that are wrong with me: I'm lazy, I'm stupid, I'm selfish, and on and on and on. Try it and see what happens.

If I close my eyes and say, "What do I have to be thankful for?" my brain will automatically start listing all the things I am thankful for: My children, my spouse, my health, my family, our warm and comfortable home, good friends who love and support me, etc: Try this experiment yourself, and see what happens.

It could be said that every time we are irritated, we are asking the wrong question. For example, you're back at that project. You can think to yourself, "Will I ever get that done?" or you can think to yourself, "If I stay focused and just do one thing at a time, will I make progress?" It may or may not happen, but the statements set the foundation for how you will proceed. One is empowering and energizing, the other leaves you stranded and feeling inadequate.

How about when your spouse leaves without a kiss goodbye. You can fret and wonder and create some ghastly scenario involving cheap champagne and hotel rooms. Or you can tell yourself that you're jumping to conclusions; that you need to be mindful that he was making a big presentation, and was distracted.

Every human contact we make is open to interpretation. Every movement is a communication and we are given the opportunity to react in any variety of ways to that movement, that verbiage. Who do you complain to in a restaurant when you don't care for a meal? Do you complain to the waiter, do you complain to the cook? Do you complain to the manager? What works is to complain to the person who can do something about it, whomever can fix the problem.

Someone once said, "Argue for your limitations, and sure enough, they're yours." I believe that's true. I don't have enough time, I don't have enough money, I don't have enough energy – they're all self defeating comments; comments that limit. The sad part is that usually they are not true at all. It's just about your interpretation, because people really do what they want to do.

Why? Why were you late? Why didn't you remember? Why are you being that way? If you want to hear fairy tales, ask someone why. You'll be taken through a wonderland of incredible dangers and pitfalls, of magic carpets and evil spells. I mean it! When you ask someone 'why,' you are asking them to give you a story that you will believe. And it'll be a doozy! It usually goes like this:

Mom: Why are you late getting home from school?

Child: Oh, I had to stay after and collect the test papers.

Mom: I see. But that would only take a couple minutes. You were thirty five minutes late. What really happened?

Child: Well, you see I was on the way home and Gary's dog was following me and Gary.

Mom: Gary and me.

Child: Yeah, Gary and me. Anyway, then it ran out into the street, and we had to go after it, then it went into the alley behind the flower shop. We couldn't find him, but then we finally found him, and he was all muddy. So, I helped Gary wash him.

Mom: What really happened?

Child: Well, these bullies were chasing me. . .

This will go on until Mom is satisfied with the answer. I'm not saying this happens all the time, but 'why' is a question that almost always brings on an attempt to match what they think you want to hear.

DON'T

I've heard lots of humorous stories that centered around the word, Don't. Say "Don't spill the milk," then get ready to mop up spilt milk. "Don't get a ticket" practically guarantees an appearance in traffic court. For some reason, the word *don't* simply does not register. It's as if people are getting only the last part of the statement, like a command, like a radio broadcast that cuts out on occasion. They seem to hear, "…spill the milk," "…get a ticket." I don't know where it comes from or why we do it, but, come on, confess, you too have done this very thing!

This *don't* phenomenon works another way, too. As soon as you say, "Don't slip on the ice," your feet fly out from under you and suddenly you're looking up at the sky.

Words can dictate our quality of life. Try this small experiment. Say the word, *happy.* Get into it for a brief moment. Notice how your body is reacting to the word. You may smile; your body may relax while you say it. Now say, *sad.* Feel how your body has changed in its reaction.

When someone asks you how you are, do you say you're fine or do you say you're doing awesome!? How do you feel when you say fine? Probably, you feel just fine! When you say you feel awesome, then you really do. You become emotionally what you speak and it affects you physically – how you walk, how you stand, even your energy level.

A LESSON

I was at a Montessori school, observing a fourth grade class, when I discovered this. It is called Rules For Getting Along:

Rules
1. Identify the problem.
2. Focus on the problem.
3. Attack the problem, not the person.
4. Listen with an open mind.
5. Treat a person's feelings with respect.
6. Take responsibility for your actions.

Fouls
1. Getting even
2. Putdowns
3. Not listening
4. Name-calling
5. Blaming
6. Making excuses
7. Not taking responsibility
8. Bringing up the past.

As I look at this list, I think to myself, if we all behaved this way every day, we wouldn't have to have communications meetings. And the energy we put into our relationships would become much more positive, much more fulfilling.

THE ENERGY OF RELATIONSHIPS

In the sixties and seventies, we called it 'vibes.' "She's got good vibes." "I didn't like the vibes there, so we left." "You're giving me good vibrations…" 'Vibes' are that sensation you get when you encounter any situation. Do you feel comfortable there? Does someone give you 'the creeps'? These are 'vibes,' the energy we feel when we encounter individuals or situations. Because energy is always moving, always being emitted, we can feel it with our own energy. We call it intuition or a little voice. Whatever we call it, it is something that goes beyond the rational, physical boundaries of our bodies.

Think back to an argument you had in the past. How did you feel afterward? Drained, worn out? That's because all your energy went into the fight, you threw it all out there to make yourself right. You were actually trying to capture another person's energy. If you won the argument, you probably felt pretty good; you captured that person's energy. If you lost the argument, then you probably felt weak, drained, somehow empty. Your psychic and physical energy were drained from you.

Now think about being in love, or when your babies were born. There you are, pouring all your energy into this beautiful person, and they are pouring all their energy into you. Love is really quite selfish, in that love makes us feel so good. So we pour our energy into this person and they pour theirs into us, because, gosh, it makes each of us feel so good! What's happening is, through this mutual energy exchange, we are being fed. Our psychic side, our souls are being enriched and nourished. We feel stronger, more in tune with the world. We see beauty in everything around us. We are kinder to others. Love gives us insight. It is truly spectacular.

So, what happens? Why do we eventually fall into some kind of rut, some roadblock to that incredible insight and light? Because we need to 'own' it. We need to own the love, the respect, and the insight. We focus completely on that other person to give us this 'high', this energy. We close ourselves off from the rest of the world, relying on that person to give us all the love and encouragement we need. We begin to feel that our loved one owes us their energy. At the same time, we somehow feel that if we don't hang onto our own energy, we might lose it all. So, we insist on having things our own way. We base all our actions on the history that we lived as children and fight to maintain those archaic and unproductive ways of the past. We suck the energy out of our loved ones, rather than feeding ours to them. We forget that to gain the prize (that wonderful, insightful energy) we must let ours flow out of us. We need to see each other in the light of beauty.

Try this simple exercise: sit across from a loved one – your spouse, your child, whomever. Gaze at them and think about how much you love them, how they are beautiful and how they are wonderful. Let your eyes go out of focus. Look at your loved one's energy, their aura, if you will, and allow your love to flow into them.

They will feel it. And you will know, because you will feel it, too. You may be doing this all the time, yet you are not making yourself aware of it. Practice loving your family. Practice pouring your energy into them. Children love doing this with Mom and Dad.

Think of it this way: When you have a family, you end up with a variety of activities. Soccer, tennis, ballet – there are times when you are using energy just getting them there. Think about your state of mind when you are shuttling everyone back and forth. Are you focused on the heavy traffic, that idiot driver in front of you? Instinctively, you want to protect your children, get them through the traffic safely. But you are focused on the *circumstance* and allowing *fear* for your children to cloud your energy. Take this time to focus on your family. Focus on the importance and privilege of the job you are doing, getting your children safely to their activities. Focus on how much you love them and want to make sure they are safe and happy. So, what if the traffic is heavy? The delays give you an extra moment to cherish their energy, their enthusiasm, and their youthful joy. What a wonderful gift you have been given! Give to your children your full heart, and you will see them prosper and grow in their love for you and the world. As an added bonus, you will find the physical energy to get through the day!

Love feeds us as surely as food does. Love gives us not only psychic energy, but physical energy as well. Think to when you were first in love. You hardly needed to eat, but food, when you did eat, tasted especially good. You were getting so much energy from the love you were giving and receiving that the need for physical, carbon-based energy was decreased. You simply didn't need it.

You might find, that, as you focus more on the energy you give and receive, you will not need to eat as much, that food will taste better, in fact, that every aspect of your life will get better. Remember the old adage, "Be careful what you wish for, you just might get it." So often, we are focused on the negative; as a result, the negative happens. Quantum physics has shown that the act of observation itself alters the results of the experiment. In other words, you *can* change the course of events simply by believing it to be so. If you believe your mate to be a philanderer, then s/he will be a philanderer. If you believe your child to be a troublemaker, s/he will be a troublemaker. It really does matter how you look at the glass, half empty or half full. So look at your loved ones with truly loving eyes, feed them the power of your love and trust. See them as truly beautiful. Then you will find that effective communication is that much easier and harmony becomes a way of life.

WHY CAN'T WE ALL JUST GET ALONG?

Our old notions and attitudes, which for the most part are not based in fact, are the anchors that can tie us down. But they are not the problem in and of themselves. How we communicate our displeasure is just as strong a barrier to true harmony and intimacy in the family. To have true harmony in our married and family lives, we need to speak with love in our hearts and reverence for each other. But often we resort to dishonest communication:

- **Agree/Disagree.** For some reason it seems essential to us, as human beings, to be 'right' all the time; that everyone agree with our viewpoint. We often argue for our own limitations, refusing to hear another point of view. We view disagreement as a lack of love and support. We allow our pride to get in the way of harmony and love.

- **Specific Listening.** Often we hear only what we want to, that which is consistent with our standards. We learn this one at a young age, particularly if the primary mode of communication in the home is nagging and cajoling. Why listen when it's always the same thing over and over? It is disrespectful, of course. And of course, the less one listens the more his partner will nag and cajole. It's a vicious cycle.

- **Justification.** We love to have a reason for everything we do. This is especially true when we have somehow violated someone else's rules. It is almost instinctive for us to justify our behavior. If our first excuse isn't accepted, we will give another excuse. We will keep on giving excuses until one is finally accepted or we have worn down our opponent.

- **Pre-judging.** This one can go both ways. On the one hand, we look for the underlying motives behind the communication. For instance, your husband calls and says he'll be late coming home from work, that he has a project to complete. Suddenly you're asking yourself what the real reason is that he will be late. Is he really going out for a beer with the boys? When we try to read motives into others' behavior we disrespect them and feed into our foolish mistrust and jealousy. On the other hand, we often hint around at something, expecting our loved ones to know what it is that we want. We challenge their dedication when we try to make them figure out the puzzle: "If you really loved me, you'd know what it is that I want." When they do not fill in the blanks to our satisfaction, we become sullen and push guilt onto them. Playing coy is selfish and destructive to a harmonious relationship.

- **Unfair Comparisons.** This can tear down a child's self esteem faster than just about anything. When children are compared to their siblings they are being held up to an impossible ideal – no two children are the same, so they cannot have the same talents, abilities, drive, intelligence or charm as their brothers and sisters. How can we say that one snowflake is more beautiful than another? We have been given such precious gifts in our children, and to compare them as if they were in some sort of contest is dis honoring that gift. When we compare our spouse to "the one that got away," or some idealized version of what we want them to be, we dishonor our loved ones and thus our selves.

● **Torment.** I know a woman who had four older brothers. They loved their little sister, but were less than gentle about her weight. They called her butterball and said they wanted the fifth child to be a boy so they could have a basketball team; instead, they got the basketball. These words were not spoken with malice, but they cut deep. As a result, the woman has had a difficult time accepting the fact that she is a large person, that she will always be large and that it is okay. We say things under the guise of humor that attack and tear down the self-esteem of others. These thoughtless words can and do hurt!

We have now discussed family; what it is and how it works. We have also covered perceptions, attitudes, and beliefs. They are formed by events, environment, knowledge and past results. We connected this up with rules, standards, and guidelines and found that stress is produced when they are violated. We looked at the development of the human being and the stages that we all go through in our attempt to grow.

So now what? What has to happen to change the rules, standards, and guidelines and bring us closer to each other? How do we break down the barriers that prevent us from living more nurturing lives? We have the power. All it takes is commitment to ourselves and to our families. The first step is to commit. Commit to wanting a happier home, a more harmonious family.

CHAPTER 8

Getting It All Together

WHAT HAS TO HAPPEN?

As far as I know, communication is the only avenue, the only opportunity to resolve any and all issues. Communication is the most powerful tool in any situation to make things right or put them in a proper perspective. It's critical that families learn to resolve disagreements without the anger and the fear and the lashing out. It is not only essential to making yourself heard, but it is essential if anyone is going to listen.

When families are in harmony, grades actually improve, stress goes down, there is much more harmony and love. There is more *self-responsibility*. Children and teens are more likely to go to their parents with issues and concerns, rather than holding it in or going to their peers. When communication is working in the home, there is better self-esteem and self-acceptance. Family ties are strengthened.

When I am working with families, I am often reminded of a cartoon I saw once in a newspaper. It showed a florist standing in the window of his shop. Across the window was written, "Fresh cut flowers. Take them home and watch them die!"

Do you think maybe the florist was unclear on the concept?! From time to time that is just what I find when I work with families, dealing with family interactions. It often seems that the families are unclear on the concept. When the concept of communication is unclear, what happens is lost affinity, people withdraw their emotions. The definition of *withdraw* is to keep back, to keep from being known.

When there is no more fear of retribution for emotions and feelings, a partnership of honesty takes place. Trust and sharing escalate. We become more open.

Remember the triangle? It consists of three sides. No matter how it is turned, the triangle stays stable. No matter how it is turned or viewed, it is stable, it is balanced. The foundation for improved communication is the same way. We must build communication on the foundation of Trust, Increased Awareness and Increased Knowledge. We need to trust that whatever we want or need will be accomplished. We must increase our awareness of those around us, and to see what they need and want. We need to increase our knowledge of the world around us as well as the methods for improving communication and harmony. Tim Gallwey uses this triangle in coaching, and effective communication is another form of coaching. This can also serve as the basis for the family meeting.

The family meeting is a wonderful place to deepen your understanding of each other, find out what rules, standards, guidelines, and boundaries each person has brought into the family. It is a place where each person can have their say, safe from retribution, secure in the knowledge that what is presented will be acknowledged and resolved in a loving environment. The family will learn consistency. The family will learn to acknowledge and support one another, to accept that acknowledgment and support. What is critical to moving on is to determine the rules under which the household will operate.

Phil Jackson, in his book, *Sacred Hoops*, made a point that wears well. He said as a young man he had pretty much his own point of view. As he got older, he realized that yes, indeed, there were two points of view; his and perhaps the person he was talking with. As he moved into coaching the great Chicago Bulls he realized that there were often eight or nine points of view, and often they all seemed to be accurate, the answer, the direction to go.

I find in working with families, that more often than not, there is only one point of view that counts: that of the parents! So many times the parents take the position that they, and only they know what's best. What is more likely is that they are simply passing on what they themselves learned as children. The same values, the same concepts, the same ideas. Meanwhile, times have changed immensely since these parents were children. Peer pressure is different. Communication is different. Satellites and computers have brought the world closer. Yet, we often foster the same notions and standards we grew up with. This is a particular problem when it comes to teenagers. Teens are people who are no longer children, but are not yet adults. Some days they act like children, some days they are so mature it scares you. But they are in a 'no man's land,' so to speak. This is where the parents' rules come into conflict with the teen's concept of what the rules should be.

DETERMINING THE STANDARDS, GUIDELINES AND RULES

The family meeting can help the family come together to determine and clarify the family's standards, guidelines, and rules. When we focus too much on the "shoulds" and "oughts", we close ourselves off to personal self-growth. I am not saying throw all the standards and rules out the window, but I am suggesting perhaps some could be replaced with an open forum, focusing on what is essential for your environment. What I am saying is that the family needs to determine together what types of behavior are acceptable and what types of behavior are not. The family needs to determine what is really important, as opposed to what has been expected in the past. This is not always an easy thing to do; in the final analysis, the parents are in charge, or ought to be. It requires an objective dissection of the rules and beliefs that supposedly support those rules. It might be a good idea for each family member to take some time and write down what they feel are the rules and how important those rules are to the family, perhaps even giving them a rating from Most Important to Least Important. It might look something like this:

Standard, Rule or Guideline	*More Important*			*Less Important*	
Always use appropriate manners	5	4	3	2	1
Bedtime is 9:00 p.m. for children	5	4	3	2	1
No dating before the age of fifteen	5	4	3	2	1
Bedrooms must be cleaned daily	5	4	3	2	1
Children must never talk back to adults	5	4	3	2	1
Family members eat supper together	5	4	3	2	1
Kissing in public is forbidden	5	4	3	2	1

The point of the exercise is to determine where the family members are coming from. You may want to enlarge this exercise with your own ideas. It helps the family to decide what the priorities are, what is essential and what can be negotiated or compromised. When each family member is clear on what is expected, then it is easier for each person to uphold their end. I cannot tell you what is important to your family. Only you can determine that. But it is necessary for each family to set their own standards, guidelines, and rules of behavior.

For example, let's look at item number 6, regarding family supper. Studies show that when families eat together at least one meal a week, stress levels go down, happiness and harmony in the household are increased. Grades tend to go up. Family members seem to rest better and they seem to be in a better mood for the most part. That's just with one meal in twenty-one. Just think of the possibilities if all meals were shared with the family. But having a rule that states that all meals must be eaten together would be a difficult one to achieve. If this is a strong rule, then the family would have to work together, to negotiate just how that would be accomplished. When all the family members' schedules are examined, is this a feasible solution? What can you do to accomplish this goal? Can schedules be changed? Can activities be cancelled or postponed? Negotiation or compromise is a process of give and take. What the family needs to focus on is the better good of the family. What will make the most difference with the family? From time to time individual differences must be given up to benefit the family unit. This is not always easy and this is why negotiation is so very important here.

Yet, it must be remembered that these negotiations are an ongoing process. In the light of ever-changing priorities, this is a conversation that must be held consistently and regularly to maintain family harmony.

The modern American family is faced with an incredible array of options. Sports, music and dance fill our children's afternoons. Parents face the demands of work and sometimes those demands conflict with the family's activities. The entire family needs to sit down together again and decide what is important. What activities can be cut back or eliminated? Can the parent do some of his or her job from home? If the child is home alone for a period of time, what is considered important enough to interrupt the parent at work? There is a big difference between important and urgent. Sometimes the urgent must take priority over the important. But if the family is what is important, then by all means, the urgent things need to be closely examined before the determination is to be made. Is that meeting with the new client urgent enough to miss your son's important baseball game? Is the overtime to make money for the trip to Disneyland more urgent than seeing your daughter run in her first important track meet? A great question to consider is: Who is in charge? You? The children? Peer pressure? Someone's schedule?

When the parents make their children, their family the most important priority, the children see that the love the parents profess is genuine. It can be a challenge for a child to believe that daddy really does love him if he never comes to his school play because of work.

The single parent has an almost insurmountable obstacle here. Often, a few hours off the paycheck can mean the difference between making the rent or not. It is almost impossible for the single parent to attend to the child, to make the child the first priority, in a sense. This is the time that effective communication is even more essential.

The bottom line here: Figure out what is important as opposed to what is urgent. Stopping to smell the roses can be incredibly difficult at times, but it needs to be done if the family is to grow and flourish. The parents must take the initiative. Because of our parental role, we need to be the ones to teach our children just how the family can accomplish what is so very important. We must teach our children well. After all, we only get one opportunity to raise that child.

PARENTS AS TEACHERS

We are the providers, the defenders, the caretakers. We are also the teachers. Every move we make, everything we do, is observed by our children. Children model after us. They do what they see, not what we tell them to do. They see us at our best and at our worst. We can talk and talk forever to our children, but if we ourselves do not live our lives the way we want them to live their lives, they will learn about hypocrisy from a front row seat. They will learn that our words mean nothing, that we are, at best confused and, at worst, liars. Children learn from our actions. We cannot take them to church on Sunday, listen to the scripture of the Good Samaritan and expect them to get anything from it if we walk over the legs of a homeless man and mumble to him, "Get a job, you bum." We cannot cheat on our income tax – with the reasoning that the government does a lousy job anyway – and expect our children to refrain from cheating on a test – with the reasoning that the teacher was doing a lousy job anyway.

We are our children's teachers. We are the example they follow. The apple never falls far from the tree. If we are to see the best in our children, we need to provide an example for them to follow. Very few adults and most children do not like to be told what to do. Coaching as opposed to telling is a huge distinction. When parents shift from telling children what to do to a position of coaching, this powerful refocus results in more mindful children, more thoughtful children, and less stress among the parents.

PARENTS AS COACHES

In our society, it's okay for children not to know any thing until they are five or six years old. If they show a certain aptitude at an early age, we call them precocious and put them on display, but for the most part, we don't expect them to do much more than stop when we say stop, eat when we say eat, and sleep when we say sleep. But as soon as they start school, we start expecting them to perform, so we start offering praise or rejection. Most of this centers around schoolwork. If the child does well in school and gets good grades, she gets praise. If she does poorly, she is rejected in some way; at least that's how it feels from their point of view. This is how parents try to manage their children – rewards for good behavior, rejection for bad. This can block the natural inclinations of children to learn. They figure it doesn't matter what they do, the parents will interpret it their way anyway. It stifles their journey of self-discovery.

Children are very intuitive and have a wonderful grasp of the obvious. They need very little in the way of instruction or direction. Children do much better when they are coached, rather than lectured. We have all done it before, 'fixing' the science project so it looks more like a report from Jet Propulsion Laboratories than a fourth grade rendering of a rocket. 'Helping' with the cookies little Jamie is making for Grandma, making them all the same size and shape, instead of allowing little Jamie to do it. Taking over on the soapbox racer so it will go faster than all the others. We get so caught up in making the child's project the best, that we take over; we make them do it a certain way. We offer tons of advice and then wonder why the child is no longer showing an interest in the project.

Imagine how you would feel if your boss came up to your desk and said, "Here, you're doing that wrong. Let me do it." You would feel small and degraded and you would probably just throw up your hands and walk away. That is just how our children feel when we do it to them. Suddenly the project is no more fun. The thrill of discovery is removed, making the project a lesson in futility.

It would be effective for the parents to back off, to allow the children to discover for themselves the best methods, the shortcuts, the improvements. Parents are a natural for the role of coach. Coaches do not do the work, they ask questions, they guide, and they illuminate. A good coach can point out the doors to success and never have to open them himself. A good coach is one who helps – through their silence or the well placed, 'what do you think?' A good coach rarely answers the questions, he only asks more, and allows the student, the player, the child to figure out the answers.

Parents are in the ideal position of being coaches. We can and must allow our children to discover for themselves the answers to their questions, to make the decisions that will help them to become better people. Acting as coaches – asking rather than telling – we can give our children the ability to grow wise as they learn to think for themselves in a loving and safe environment.

COACHING

Good coaching is organized around questions. The good coach can ask a series of questions, inviting the 'student' to explore the possibilities, and allowing the 'student' to discover a different point of view for him or herself. The good coach will drop hints, but give little feedback in order to exercise a muscle that has had little or no use in the past. Good coaching is not telling. Good coaching is measured in the success of someone else. Good coaching takes patience; it's much easier to jump in and tell someone how to do something, rather than leading them on a path of self-discovery.

There is a distinction between management and coaching. Management is all pretty much about telling someone what to do. Coaching asks and invites. In the family environment, the most effective type of family harmony is a combination of management and coaching. Management includes getting to school on time, daily chores, study time. Coaching would take a different tactic. Coaching would ask questions to guide the child into taking responsibility. "What would it take to make sure your daily chores are done?"

I had the great privilege of working with Tim Gallwey, author of

The Inner Game of Tennis, and R.B (Bob) Young Jr., former CEO of Lockheed Engineering and Management Services Co., Inc. in a two-year coaching program for my clients. At one time Bob had seven Lockheed presidents, along with another ten managers reporting to him while he oversaw the efforts and direction of twenty-five thousand employees. Tim, while in school, had served as captain of the Harvard tennis team. Based on his experience on the tennis court, Tim developed a whole field of coaching in the business world that had not been addressed to any extent until he came along.

The triangle is the most stable geometric figure known. Its three sides work interdependently to provide a complete and stable environment. The coaching we provided required three elements.

- *Trust.* Trust doesn't mean you won't make mistakes, rather trust involves believing that the coaching is going in the right direction. The student must trust that the coach will work for the good of the student.

- *Willingness.* The student needs to have a desire to change, to progress, to learn something new, to grow.

- *Awareness.* The student must be willing to open his or herself to learning. The student must be willing to 'not know', so to speak, thus allowing knowledge and awareness in.

Many people say they want coaching, but often what they really want is someone who will agree with their point of view, who will help them justify their actions. Coaching requires that one put down their pre-conceived notions, step outside of how it's always, that they are look at something differently, to receive the contributions of others.

The Coaching Triangle *must* be in place before there can be any effective change. When a child goes to a parent with a question or a concern, they are opening the door to a wonderful opportunity. By coming to the parent, the child is indicating trust, *and* a willingness to hear what you have to say. This is such a powerful starting point; the child has opened the door with a question rather than the parent opening the door with a suggestion.

Now the parent must ask in their own way, is the child willing and ready to increase awareness? Is the child ready and willing to look in a different direction, to feel uncomfortable, to be disagreed with?

Good coaching works with perception, awareness and compassion. Good coaching requires intuition. When I coach people, I don't know the exact

Magic happens when a family is in relationship!

questions to ask. I simply listen carefully to the responses. Each response leads to the next question. Soon the 'student' will see, in their own responses, an insight that will help them achieve their goal. You, as the coach, don't have to have answers. Just keep asking questions until something "clicks," until the light bulb goes on.

Telling people how to do something is lousy coaching. It takes patience to coach. It takes time. Telling is much easier than coaching but the cost can be very high. Good coaching is not about a conclusion; it's about a journey. It's about support along the way. Good coaching not only includes participation; it might result in delegation. As I said earlier, the 'student' must be willing to be coached about a particular situation. It's not good form to ask someone it they are committed. Of course they are committed. The commitment may look different from day to day, but the simple virtue of their presence on this Earth is evidence of their commitment.

COACHING EXERCISE

Tim showed me this interesting and enlightening exercise. I've used it in seminars and in personal coaching sessions. The exercise can take anywhere from five to fifteen minutes. You can do this alone, or as a coach.

Start tapping your fingers on some surface. It can be a table or your knee. It doesn't matter. Just keep tapping. Do not talk during this time. Every couple of minutes, ask yourself (or your 'student'), "What are you learning?"

I have received a wide variety of answers to that question. Some people have noticed their impatience and frustration that time seems to pass so slowly. Some people have discovered a song in their tapping. Some found themselves tapping out a code. Some became calm, some became bored. Others became sleepy. All of it hooked up to something else, and without exception, it all revealed something about them.

The point of this exercise is that one can always learn, and one can always be coached about anything, anytime, anywhere. One of the ingredients revealed was the willingness of the individual to be coached. Could the person trust me enough to continue tapping on a table for five minutes or longer?

GOALS

Once you have determined that the individual is ready for coaching, it is essential to get clear on the goals. The goal in baseball is to get the ball over the fence. In tennis, the goal is to keep the ball inside the fence. Then there are the variables. How hard is the ball hit? What type of equipment are you using to hit the ball? How is the wind? Is the sun in your eyes? Are you feeling tired or do you have a lot of energy? There are some absolutes: the size of the court, the size of the ball, the surface being played. Clarity about the goal is perhaps the most important part of good coaching. Without it, the coaching becomes nebulous and lacks direction. The 'student' might be learning something, but it is probably not going to help the situation as intended.

Being coached can be an uncomfortable situation. People usually don't like to be reminded of their own ineptitude, but that's often what happens in coaching. It's supposed to happen. It gives the 'student' the opportunity to see for him or herself what is standing between them and their goals.

In coaching, it is useful to stay within a 'neutral zone.' By that I mean, don't give a lot of feedback, either good or bad. When you give a lot of feedback, you are taking the coaching into a direction that you, the coach, want the lesson to go, rather than the direction that the 'student' must discover for themselves.

Quantum Physics has shown us that simple observation can, and does, change the outcome of the experiment. When we assign a degree of competency to the subject (that was a great shot), we tip the scales in the direction that we wish them to go.

I would watch Tim coach people on the tennis court. He would have his students focus on the mechanics of the game. When the racket made contact with the ball, the student would say, "Hit." When the ball bounced on the court, the student would say, "Bounce." Whether the ball hit inside the court or bounced over the fence, Tim would make no comment on the shot itself. He might ask the student, "How did that feel?" Soon the students would be concentrating on the physical feeling of a 'good' or 'bad' shot rather than the emotions attached to it. The students, on their own, figured out whether they were doing better or worse. They knew what the game was. The focus was no longer on the 'win or lose' of the situation, but on the mechanics of doing whatever it took to get the job done.

This is where many breakdowns occur in the family. There is too much attention on making the situation 'right' and not enough on practicality. What is standing in the way of the goal? How do we go about achieving the goal? What has to change? Instead of asking, we tend to tell the answers even before the student is even aware of the questions. We get into telling people what ought to be, what they ought to do, what they ought not to do. Another way to say it is with the two words, 'should' and 'don't' that get in the way of awareness. Yet, another way to say it is, our rules get in their way.

I am convinced that anybody can coach anyone else about any particular subject, without having any knowledge in that field. For instance, Tim, who is tone deaf and cannot read music, was retained by the Boston Philharmonic Orchestra to improve the quality of their music. Tim did just that. The improvement was so profound that the conductor sang Tim's praises and when the orchestra received a major award, they gave the credit to Tim.

Coaching is a two-way street. In any insightful relationship, the role of coach and the role of student are often flipped. The 'student' suddenly can and will offer insights that the coach had never even considered. So as coach, you must be willing to set your ego aside and be receptive to the lessons you, too, will learn.

I was once called in to coach a young man who was getting very poor grades in high school. Testing revealed he was an intelligent boy, and had no major difficulties in his life. He'd been tutored, he'd been punished, and he'd been placed on restrictions. Still, he could never seem to get his grades out of the basement. So I was called in to coach. He and I sat down and I began asking him questions. What is your school like? Tell me about your teachers. The questioning went on until I discovered that he sometimes studied with his best friend who was getting straight 'A's.' I asked about his best friend's study habits and why he liked studying with his buddy. The first answer was obvious: "He gets to listen to loud music when he studies. My parents say loud music will distract me. I can only listen to mellow music."

We'd discovered earlier that the boy rarely finished any of his tests. He spent too much time on each question, searching his mind for the right answer, right now. Since not all of the questions got answered, his grades were artificially skewed. I asked about how his friend took tests. "He goes through and answers all the questions he's sure of. If there's time left, he goes back and answers the questions he skipped. He says a lot of the time there's a question that will answer the question you can't remember. And he never changes an answer." The boy suddenly realized that if he took tests the way his friend did, he would increase his grade by the simple virtue of finishing the test.

His parents agreed to let go of the music issue, so he had an environment in which he was comfortable. With only three weeks left to the semester, he raised all of his grades at least one full grade, and in two of his classes, his grades went up two full grade points. He thought it all through by himself. All I did was ask the questions that helped him discover an insight. His and his family's willingness to change made it possible for him to recognize the insights he received in that brief, ten-minute coaching session.

Good coaching requires that you not focus on the solution. Rather, focus on the barriers that are preventing the 'student' from finding a solution. An outstanding consultant and friend, Joan Garbo and I were sitting next to a pool one day, enjoying the sunshine and the splashing of children in the pool. There were several boys and one girl racing the length of the pool. We were especially taken by the girl, who was a good swimmer, but who could not seem to beat the boys. Soon, Joan started a conversation with her. She asked about the girl's swimming skills. "Do you want to beat the boys?" Joan asked. "Of course," said the girl. "How come you can't beat the boys?" The girl, in her self-limiting belief said, "I can't get enough air." "If you got enough air, would you be able to beat the boys?" "Sure," said the girl, "But I don't know how I can get more air."

Joan then asked the girl if she would be willing to try something. She shrugged her shoulders and agreed. Joan invited her to take a lap and count how many times she takes a breath as she goes across the pool. The girl tried it. Needless to say, by the second race, the girl was beating the boys and handily. Joan, by inviting the girl to focus on the air she *was* getting, shifted the focus away from the air she was not getting. The girl was then able to remove the barrier and the solution revealed itself.

I have coached thousands of people, in countless situations, over the years. I've coached people on their jobs, on their school work and on their relationships. I've coached people about their weight, their smoking and their drug addictions. I've coached businesses, I've coached individuals, and I've coached families. It makes no difference what the subject or issue is, coaching is simply a method of helping others see for themselves. It is a path to insight. As a coach, I do not have to be an expert in the field of weight control, drug addiction or football. My job is to listen attentively and ask questions.

I've seen families reconcile major differences and I've seen failing businesses turn around, all due to coaching. I don't think I have ever run into a problem that can't be resolved with coaching. Remember that coaching is simply helping someone get clear on what is not working so that they can focus on what will work. Coaching is a method that takes the emotional attachment to the situation out of the way, and creates the environment that leads to new solutions, new creations, and new ideas. This is where self-discovery is critical.

SELF-DISCOVERY VS. SELF-IMPROVEMENT

I don't think there's any such thing as self-improvement. Self-improvement implies that there is something 'wrong' with us, with our *'inner-self'*. There's nothing 'wrong' with our 'self', it's just a matter of self-discovery. If we seem as if we are improving, it is simply because we are becoming more aware, more insightful. Self-improvement implies that we are stupid. Self-discovery implies that we are letting go of ignorance.

There is a big difference between stupidity and ignorance. Ignorance is not knowing something. Ignorance means that you have not been exposed to a certain learning situation. Stupidity is something you know is not good for you and you go ahead and doing it anyway. You can be ignorant, but you can't be stupid. The things you do, knowing that are detrimental, are the things that are stupid. Stupid is an action. Ignorance is a state.

Say you smoke cigarettes. You would have to have been on another planet for the last twenty years if you don't know that smoking cigarettes is harmful to your health. You know that cigarettes are a sure path of destruction. Yet you smoke anyway. You are not ignorant. Nor are you stupid. It could be said that you simply engage in a stupid habit.

Children, not having the life experience of adults, are, many times, ignorant. They certainly aren't stupid. They simply don't have an instinctive knowledge of how to resolve certain issues without the background of awareness in certain areas. They don't come out of the womb knowing how to handle themselves socially, how to solve problems, how to accomplish something new. That's why they have parents. Parents are the teachers and coaches. And we can use our role as teachers to be educators (who tell you what to think), or we can be coaches (who ask you how, who ask you to think). We can manage our children into robots or we can point them on their way to an incredible journey: life. Coaching, while a seemingly simple subject, is certainly an engaging one, and a challenge to master. Yet, to help our children on their way, there is much more involved than just coaching.

SHARING RESPONSIBILITY

It has been said that it takes an entire community to raise a child. I agree. A child's grades in school are not just his own. The grade reflects more than the child's ability to grasp the subject. It reflects the curriculum: Is it age appropriate; is it challenging enough to interest the child but not so difficult that he is overwhelmed by it? It reflects on the teacher: how well does the teacher know the subject? How is the subject taught? It reflects on the parents: what is the family attitude toward education? What assistance, if any does the child receive at home? This by no means takes the responsibility off the shoulders of the child. What I am saying is that for the child to be able to be responsible, the adults involved must also be responsible.

Blaming the system, blaming the parents, blaming the child has no redeeming attributes. Blame effects no change. Blame cannot fix what is not working. Only when everyone gets past the blame and realizes that the responsibility is on their shoulders, will change take place. The child needs to say, "I will take 'self-responsibility' for making sure my homework is handed in on time." The teacher needs to say, "I will take responsibility for approaching the child when he needs assistance." The school board needs to say, "We will take responsibility for making sure there are current and accessible resources for quality education." And parents need to say, "We will take responsibility to make sure our child is given the time, the energy and the environment to make learning not only possible, but enriching."

When we take responsibility for the quality of our lives and the lives of our children, we empower ourselves. We are no longer victims. By making ourselves responsible, we proclaim ourselves, and we have no need to fear. Our society has been in turmoil as more and more are using government assistance. Since the Great Depression, we have become a society in which accountability is often completely disregarded. We allow others to take care of things. We scream long and hard about our rights, but few are actually willing to take the responsibility that must go with those rights. A woman spills hot coffee in her lap and the company that brewed the coffee must pay her two million dollars. Every day we hear how the tobacco companies have to pay out to the families of smokers, who, for years bought the product, were fully aware of the dangers of tobacco. As a nation we abdicate our responsibilities then moan and groan about how the government is taking away our rights.

The home situation is very much the same. In 88 percent of the households, there is some version of "rights versus responsibility" struggle. Teens are especially good at this. How many times have you heard the phrase, "You treat me like I'm a little baby!" Teens sometimes forget that as they are becoming older they need to take on more 'responsibility' to correspond with the additional 'rights' they want and indeed expect. Making sure those 'responsibilities' are carried out is made easier when the consequence for a lack of 'responsibility' is a lack of 'rights.' It is easy for a teen to 'forget' their 'responsibilities' when life is waiting, so exciting and promising. Of course, it's just as easy for a parent to forget they promised the teen they could use the car (a privilege not a right) only if the garage is cleaned up.

One way to teach responsibility is to correlate it directly with rights. If the garbage is taken out regularly, then playtime is allowed after dinner. If the goal is an overnight with friends, the means to the goal is dusting and vacuuming. If Janet wants use of the car, perhaps Janet must provide the funds for the fuel she uses and for her insurance. If David wants to play on the football team, maybe he must maintain a 'B' grade average.

Each right comes with a corresponding responsibility. That way, the incentive for a desired behavior is clearly delineated. When the child is not responsible, the consequence is the removal of the right. It is an effective form of discipline, probably the most effective form. And it can be used with children as young as two.

Of course one of the most powerful ways to teach responsibility and the consequences of one's actions is by participating in your child's life.

PARTICIPATING IN YOUR CHILD'S LIFE

Wanting all the best for our children, we tend to overbook them. We give them lessons: ballet, karate, tennis, gymnastics, skiing, swimming…the list is endless. We put them into groups, church groups, scouts, 4H. Every minute of their day is filled. Not only can this be incredibly costly, it robs us of time we could be sharing with them, or time they could use for daydreaming or contemplation.

I have a friend who was a ski instructor at a major destination ski resort in California. She told me about how she would take children for full-day lessons, skiing with them, lunching with them, playing and talking with them until their parents gathered them at the end of the day. For every class that she taught, there would be at least one child whose only wish was to ski with his or her parents. My friend would cry for the children who were brought to the mountain for a family vacation, only to be placed in yet another class while the parents went gallivanting around the mountain.

My friend's heart ached for one child in particular. This little girl had been in ski classes for the first four days of the family's vacation. They had one day left and all the little girl wanted to do was to ski with her mother. My friend met the mother at the end of the day and explained the child's progress. The mother patted the child with pride. Then my friend came to her suggestions, "Lizzy has done a great job and has learned a lot in the past few days. It would be great for her to have a day off from the lessons so she can ski with you and show you how much she has accomplished." The mother stopped patting the child, looked down at her and snapped, "So, you think you finally got your own way, huh?" My friend was aghast! She wanted to scream at the woman. My friend, a single mother, who could think of nothing she wanted more than to be able to ski with her own daughter, had met someone who did not want to be with their child at all. With all the money and advantage, this poor little rich girl was incredibly, incredibly alone.

As for my friend, she learned an invaluable lesson. She finished out the season, fulfilling her commitment to the ski school, but did not go back. Instead, she found work she could do from her home, gave up the season passes and gave her time to her own child.

If we send our children to all these lessons and classes, we can't wonder why they never come to see us after they have grown. Remember the old song, *Cat's Cradle*: *"...As I hung up the phone it occurred to me, he'd grown up just like me, my boy was just like me."*[4] To keep the family connected, we must make that connection, we must strengthen that connection and we must protect that connection with every ounce of our being. And there is nothing so powerful to connecting as learning how to conduct a successful "family meeting."

CHILDREN AS LEADERS

The Family Connection process is a simple one. When Sue and I began *The Family Connection Meetings*, I initially served as the facilitator. But who actually provided the balance and really helped to create a safe environment was Sue. This happened for two reasons. First, she had a woman's touch, a woman's intuition and a woman's compassion. Second, Jerran and Andy were her sons. Over the years, as we continued the family meetings, Sue was consistently the stabilizing influence. I would say that this is the case in most family meetings. The mother is very influential in providing the bridge of safety and compassion that allows the rest of the family to communicate effectively using this process.

Soon, Jerran and Andy took over the role of facilitator. It was then that the meetings really took off. With the children as facilitators, we found that we as adults were called upon to be even more responsible. The boys were able to bring a freshness to the process, an innocence, if you will. I have encouraged this practice with all families; I strongly recommend that all "family meetings" be led by one of the children.

Aside from the obvious responsibility, children also learn leadership. Children as young as seven or eight are able to lead the meeting and to derive the benefits that the role offers. When children are the leaders, they see for themselves the importance of keeping order. They find out about responsibility, they learn the importance of diplomacy. Children who have led family meetings show an increase in self-esteem. They see themselves as contributors, vital members of the family team. When they themselves are responsible for the boundaries within the meeting, they are more appreciative of the boundaries that their parents have established. And finally, the child who leads the meetings is more likely to pay attention and really listen to what is transpiring in the meeting.

I related to you at the beginning of the book about Herb and his son, Hunter. I had worked with his family and helped them establish *The Family Connection* meeting in their home. They had several children of varying ages. The youngest, Hunter, was about three or four when the family began to use the process. When children are very small like that, I do not recommend that they be required to attend the meetings. Certainly they should be invited, but they need to be allowed to wander in and out of the meeting at will, as long as it is not disruptive. Hunter had been wandering in and out of the meetings and the family really hadn't thought twice whether the boy was paying attention or not.

There came a time when the grandmother took ill and died. The family was in deep grief when little Hunter called a family meeting. They sat together as this small child led them into a discussion about death, about loss, and about the faith we find through such passages. Before long the family was hugging, laughing, crying – sharing the beautiful memories of life with Grandma. And it was the child who had led them to each other, to begin the healing and celebration of life.

Children can make excellent leaders. They have not yet grown jaded to the events around them; they see with fresh eyes and open minds. Children are able to offer solutions that may seem simplistic, yet when instituted are very effective. Children can and should be in charge of their lives, within parental boundaries, and receive guidance and coaching from the parents.

Not long after Sue's divorce, Andy, then in second grade, found himself having great difficulty focusing from day to day. His behavior in class was disruptive. He argued with his teachers, his report card was peppered with low grades. Because of his disruptive behavior patterns, he'd been separated from the rest of his class. His desk was in the back of the room facing the back wall in the hopes that his behavior would not bother the other children.

Realizing that a lot of his actions were a result of the hurt and pain of the divorce, we tried everything; we tried patience, we tried compassion. We tried grounding him, taking away privileges, nagging and cajoling; we even tried bribery. Nothing worked. Andy's behavior in school was not changing. Finally we struck upon an idea. We realized that we were trying to be responsible for Andy's education in a way that only he could be responsible. So we sat down in a family meeting and explained to him that we had made mistakes, that, after all it was *his* education, and if he wanted to spend the next year in the second grade again, it was alright with us. He asked what we meant. We explained that we'd gotten notes and met with his teacher and that it was her viewpoint that if Andy was unable to change his behavior and get his grades up, she could not recommend him to move on to the third grade. This, of course, got Andy's attention. Up to then I don't think he realized what was really at stake.

I think he thought at first that this was yet another method of interacting with him. He was probably waiting for the other foot to fall. As he sat there and we answered his questions, he finally realized that we meant it. He realized that school was his job, his responsibility and that we had stepped in, attempting to take away some of that responsibility. We set some boundaries. We told him we would stop nagging him about school. We told him that if he brought notes home from the teacher we would, of course read them, but we wouldn't overreact to them; we would simply let him know what the latest turn of events were. We took our anger, our irritations, and our overreactions out of the scene and put it back to Andy. After all, it was his problem, his responsibility. While we were compassionate and wanted it to be another way, we, his parents, knew at this time this is what we had and this was how we would handle it.

I think it was a relief to Andy. He knew it would be a little safer to be around us and he knew that if he did get in trouble at school, he wouldn't get in trouble at home. We assured him of our concern; we committed to doing anything that we knew to do. We assured him that we loved him and would continue to love him no matter what his grades were. In our way, we attempted to help him see that there was a difference between him and his grades; that he was not his grades. There was this circumstance called 'grades,' and it was separate from his '*inner-self.*' He simply had a problem called his grades. We promised that we would respect him by allowing him to be responsible for the consequences of his own actions, whether it was having his desk turned away from the rest of the class or another year in second grade. Andy accepted what we told him and no more was said about it.

A few weeks passed and we heard nothing from him about his school time. Notes came home regarding missing assignments and talking during class, but we'd made a promise to Andy and we stuck to that promise. We would sign the notes, let him know what we were signing, but we didn't nag him and we didn't embarrass him about it.

One day Andy came home and said, "Can I tell you about school?" We said, "Are you sure you want to have a conversation about it. You know it's okay if you don't. We are, after all, trying not to be involved and let you work it out for yourself." He said no, he wanted to talk to us about school and wanted to know if we'd listen to him. He seemed very determined to let us know what had happened. Not knowing what to expect, we sat down to listen.

Andy stood a little straighter. He puffed out his chest, and with a big smile on his face, proudly announced he had gotten a 'B' on his spelling test, a 'B' on his history pop quiz, and, because his behavior had improved so much, he was invited to return his desk to the main population of the class.

Andy was proud. He had seen that his actions were hurting no one but himself and that his actions spoke volumes about him as a person. Andy knew he was a good kid, he just needed to see what he was capable of doing. Andy changed his own behavior. We did not change it for him, since neither Sue or I had the power, authority, or right to change him. Once he was given the opportunity to rise to the occasion and solve his own problems, he did. We rarely had any more problems with him at school. I am proud to say that Andy completed his college education with a 'B+' average.

The lesson was a good one for a child of Andy's age. Andy wanted and needed to engage in a task that he could carry through to completion. This is a time that a child needs to feel accomplishment, achievement, cooperation and competition.

Have you ever watched as your seven year-old plays with dish soap and water? They explore the different viscosity of the mixture, they make bubbles and add food coloring. When the mixture is just right and the child gets good bubbles, notice the satisfaction and pride as they blow those bubbles and watch them float on the breeze. The entire process is a great experiment.

Andy's great experiment was his schooling. He was given the opportunity to set his own boundaries. After all, the boundaries that had been established for him had not proven successful. He was allowed to succeed or fail on his own, without the pressure of having to live up to the standards set by his parents or by his teacher. The standards he needed to live up to were his own. It was when he had that perspective, that choice, that he realized the boundaries and standards that others had established actually had merit. He was able then to see that it was in his best interests to adhere to those standards. But he needed to find out about it on his own.

We need to welcome the child, to make the child great, to acknowledge them and listen to them. To welcome children doesn't just mean allow them in the room. It does not ascribe to the old adage, "Children should be seen and not heard." When we welcome our children, we validate them. We show them that their ideas, their thoughts, their opinions are worthwhile. When we welcome a child, we listen to their ideas and consider them seriously. When we welcome a child we show respect and honor.

We spoke earlier about standards and rules and what guidelines the family would operate with. These rules depend on your family values. To enhance and enrich the family in these values the concepts of support, respect, and communication must be adhered to. This requires commitment. A commitment to the values of your family is essential for the processes success. This total commitment ensures that relationships are nurtured and satisfied at their optimum level.

CHAPTER 9

Guidelines for the Family Meeting

For the family meeting to be effective, there must be guidelines. It is essential that the environment of the meeting is conducive to change and growth. For anything to be accomplished all the members of the meeting need to feel safe, to know that whatever they say will be listened to with thoughtfulness and care, that their opinions are valid and that the people they speak with are trustworthy. The family meeting is not about getting everybody in agreement. Just as all the stars in the heavens are different, our viewpoints are different. The family meeting is about resolving those differences, eliminating the conflicts, compromising if necessary. The members need to remember that it is okay to disagree. Remember, it's not what happens to you, it's what you do about it.

As I travel around the country, lecturing and interacting with families, I get a lot of questions. Probably, the question I am asked most often is some version of, "Sonny, why are relationships so hard? How can one minute be so great, and the next so rotten?" There are a lot of answers to this, from what psychologists tell us, and, of course, there are endless opinions.

Let me tell you a story:

I was invited to sit down and work with a family that was having a lot of difficulties. Soon after I began the meeting, I realized that in this family it was not safe to speak up. The ten year-old daughter began to open up, and she did it beautifully. But when I looked at her father, I could see that he was uncomfortable. I saw what was happening. He did not like what she was telling him about his habit of yelling. Bless her heart; she had a lot of courage. She had been frightened to bring the subject up. When she had tried in the past, it only resulted in more yelling from her father. She knew that the subject was not a safe one, but in the family meeting, she was safe, and she could address the issue.

Meanwhile, the father was concerned about looking good in front of his family, about being right, about being in control. He took his daughter's remarks personally.

Up until this family meeting, the child felt repressed. She was afraid to open up to him about his yelling, because he would only yell more. Since she could not open up about that, she could not open up about other issues. Despite the fact that he had

The mind is like a parachute – it only works when it's open

told her many times that she could tell him anything, she knew that she could not. Subconsciously, she felt that if she upset him, he would take his love away, even abandon her.

She had run up against his attitudes, his beliefs, his rules that children should be seen and not heard. Of course, he got that little gem of wisdom from his parents. With all this emotional baggage, he perceived that his daughter was threatening his authority as a parent, that she was being defiant. Once he saw through the family meeting what his attitude was costing his daughter, he was able to let go of that notion, that attitude or belief and create a new standard with his family. When I left, this was a much different family than when I had arrived!

When you utilize*The Family Connection* process, you learn how to provide a safe environment where no one is afraid to speak their mind. You will overcome the emotional baggage from the past and have true freedom of expression – all the time!

There's a great little exercise that I've often used with families as well as in the workplace, that has always helped open up the space, to make the environment safe and to open people's hearts before they start the process. I call it, "What do you appreciate, like, or love about your life?"

One member would open it up by asking, "What do you appreciate, or really like, or even love about your life?" This question can be more specific: What do you like about school? What do you appreciate about our new home? What do you really like about soccer? In other words, ask a simple, direct question. Love means many things to many people. Some people talk about how they love food, then in the next breath they say they love their cat! The point of this exercise is to get people in touch with their feelings, their affinities and the things they appreciate, like, and love. Often the most effective question of all is, "What do you most love about your family?" It's a great question and a great starting point for the family meetings.

The guidelines are as follows:

1) **A Safe Environment** . Safe means any family member, especially the child, can say anything to another family member and it will be listened to, without interruption. There will be times when things will be difficult to say or to hear. There will definitely be disagreements. But no matter what it is, the speaker needs to feel safe in saying it. The speaker must know that there will be no reprisals or adverse consequences. While there may be need for action, the messenger must not be punished.

2) **No zingers or putdowns.** All family members are to be supported. Do not use humor to put someone down, as with the girl with the older brothers. Do not subject members to ridicule or embarrassment. There is no place for the nasty little asides and cutting comments: "When you were late yesterday, *like you always are...*" It adds baggage to the communication and takes the focus off what is really being discussed. It adds guilt and demeans the recipient of the communication.

3) **No explaining.** No one gets the opportunity to explain his or her situation. This is a tough challenge. Explanations and reasons for our actions or inaction take up most of our meaningful conversation. Why we did or didn't do something is not the issue here. The issue is that something did or didn't happen and because of that, someone else feels somehow violated. We cannot change history, we cannot go back in time for a 'do over.' All we can do is accept the responsibility and work

with others to resolve the situation. In more than twenty years of working with people, I have seen explanations almost always take a defensive posture. In an effort to 'be right,' the accuracy of the story begins to fade, the accused becomes the accuser then there is no resolution at all. By taking explanations out of the equation, the issues can be handled more efficiently and accurately when based on the five points: who, when, where, what happened, and, I felt…

For example, if I were interacting with an eight year-old about his room, I might say: "Billy, yesterday afternoon in your room, after you had agreed to clean it up, I went in with you and found it to be an absolute mess, I felt frustrated, annoyed and at my wit's end." This statement covers the five points: who, what, when, where, and how I felt. Now, if we are adhering to the model, Billy gets to say something like, "Okay, Dad, I'll clean it." In the beginning, Billy might use this time to give me reasons for not cleaning his room. "I got too busy," "I was waiting for clean sheets from Mom," or other such responses. Billy would naturally want to defend his inaction. They are probably all reasonable excuses and explanations. That's the very reason we interrupt the stories – so that we don't get into a side conversation that will make no difference. After all, regardless of his story, the bottom line is that Billy did not do what he promised to do. That's the real issue. Not all the stories and excuses. The facilitator might say then, "No pass. Billy, those are excuses and justifying. You just get to say, 'I understand,' or 'I hear you.'" If Billy is the facilitator, Mom or Dad might step in and remind Billy of the guidelines.

4) **Everyone stays in the meeting.** We discovered this essential guideline when we used the process at home. No matter how emotional the situation may be, no matter how angry everyone is, NO ONE LEAVES THE ROOM! Resolve the issue, smooth the conflict and get back into harmony. If we cannot walk out the door every time we are displeased, we work harder to resolve the issues. There can be no compromises if there is only one concerned partner trying to compromise. It is like a single hand clapping. Stay in the fray. The storm will clear and you will be left with the golden rainbow of promise.

5) **Assign a recorder.** It is best in the beginning to have an adult to serve as recorder. Because the steps of the meeting require that we come back to issues, it is necessary to write things down. It also serves as a record for the review of requests, promises, and solutions. It is usually best to have an adult or one of the older children act as a recorder. This also serves as a record for the review of requests, promises, and solutions as you will see later in this process.

REQUEST	BY WHOM	TO WHOM	SOLUTION	DUE DATE FOR PROMISE
Billy clean room	Dad	Billy	No toys out, no clothes on floor	Tomorrow 10/17
Be home on time for help with science project	Susie	Dad	BE THERE!	Mon. and Wed this week

At the request time, Dad would make the request to Billy to get his room cleaned. They would agree to the solutions and to a due date. That would be the end of the conversation. Dad would not embarrass Billy, they would not dwell on it. After all, this is part of Billy's responsibility. There is no need to go any further. At the next family meeting, the tracking form would be brought out and the promises reviewed. Did Billy clean his room on time and to the agreed conditions? If so, mark it off. If not, the issue needs further discussion. The tracking form eliminates confusion and keeps everyone clear on the results and expectations of the communication and reduces problems in this area.

6) **No rehashing.** Handle the issues of only those present at the meeting, and handle them during the meeting. There will be actions that will need to take place outside the meeting, but when it comes to the details of the issues presented, don't mess with them outside the meeting, unless this was a logical conclusion reached in the meeting itself. This could violate the promise of safety. Each member needs to know that their private feelings, their issues will be held in esteem and in confidence. Speaking about someone else, especially if they are not in attendance, is gossip and is not to be tolerated.

Remember, *Follow all the guidelines!* Omitting just one item can hamper the success of a meeting. It's like dialing a number on the telephone.

You can dial and dial all day long, but if one number is incorrect or left out, you will never get through.

I recommend that the family meet each week for about four or five weeks in a row. This allows the old problems to be resolved, and helps the family grow accustomed to the process. Hold the meeting around the kitchen table or in a comfortable room that is free of distractions. Hold the meeting when all members can be present, and when there are no other pressing engagements. Cancel other plans if you have to. Let your family be your first priority.

A meeting may be held any time a family member feels the need for one. After a time, you will find that the need for family meetings will decrease, as the members begin to use the techniques in their daily lives. Continue to have the meetings, though. It is a great time to touch base with each other and it is always wonderful to spend time in the fellowship and love of the family.

THE MEETING PROCESS

STAGE 1: DELIVERING PROBLEMS, CONCERNS AND UPSETS

Stage 1 of *The Family Connection* meeting focuses on Problems, Concerns, and Irritations. This is the most challenging part of the meeting. If this first stage is not handled appropriately, it is likely that Stage 2 and Stage 3 will also suffer. Until Problems, Concerns, and Irritations are expressed, listened to and the energy around them diminished, it will be almost impossible to develop Solutions or Acknowledgments that the family can hear, accept or relate to with their full support.

THE ACTUAL PROCESS

The child who is the meeting leader/facilitator would begin by reciting the guidelines. These may not always be necessary in later meetings. However, brief reminders are a good way to jump-start meetings. Remember, everyone must agree to them.

The leader/facilitator turns to the left or the right and begins by asking each person, "Is it safe for you in the meeting today?" If everyone responds that it is safe – meaning anything can be spoken and will be listened to by each member present – the leader/facilitator again begins with the original person and asks, "Do you have any Problems, Concerns, or

Irritations to communicate?" This begins the first round.

If someone isn't safe, it means there is a family member in the meeting he/she has concerns about. If this happens, the leader/facilitator asks, "What has to happen for it to be safe for you?" Working with this question, the entire family must be willing to assure the hesitant person that it is safe to say anything, without worry or further consequences. This may require some time and patience.

With safety resolved, the leader/facilitator again resumes with the original person, asking, "Do you have any Problems, Concerns, or Irritations you now want to communicate?" Here is where it really works to have everything written down! The family member who goes first begins with his/her completed worksheet.

The leader/facilitator should go around the circle, in one direction, left or right, addressing one Problem, Concern, or Irritation per person. This part of the process will continue until all of the members have communicated all of their Problems, Concerns, or Irritations. One person may have only two or three, while another may have many more. When a member is finished (has no more Problems, Concerns, or Irritations) he/she will say, "I pass," until everyone is passing (including the leader/facilitator).

WORKSHEET MODEL

1. **Who** is the communication to?

2. **When** did the incident happen?

3. **Exactly where** did this incident take place?

4. **Exactly what happened**, without a story, putdowns or zingers. If any of these negatives arise, the leader/facilitator should say, "Stop," or, "No Pass; please start that communication over."

    The first few meetings are likely to provide a lot of opportunities for correction. Members will tend to tell a story and may even interrupt others, which is very normal. But this behavior does not work and must not be allowed in a successful *Family Connection* process.

5. **How I feel** about the incident. In the Appendix at the end of this book is a list of words to help family members express clearly and honestly how they feel.

This is probably a great place for mother to be jumping in with coaching, when appropriate. Mothers tend to have more patience. They are more intuitive and have special insights. They often have more compassion during a child's learning processes.

Remember, these guidelines are here for a reason. The bigger purpose, the bigger picture is to have a successful meeting. The guidelines, when written down, can seem very rigid and sometimes even harsh. That is certainly not the intent, nor is it the result that will be produced. During the earlier meetings it is okay to bend the rules a bit. What you want is a successful meeting. Sometimes it takes a little practice. More important than the rules is having the result turn out, having the family communication and relationship to be able to speak about uncomfortable issues and be safe. No adverse consequences should be made for speaking one's mind, or the child will probably never again feel that it's safe to express his or herself.

Let's look at another example. Perhaps eleven year-old Elaine has a communication for her mother. It would go something like this:

"Mom (who), yesterday afternoon (when), when you didn't come home (where) to pick me up for the softball game (what) like you said you would, I felt (how I felt) sad, and not important to you." The mother's response would be an acknowledgment of the issue, "I hear you," or "I'm sorry, it won't happen again."

Elaine or Mom or even another family member may have a request regarding this problem in the second round. That person would say, "I have a request regarding this." The recorder would then write down that there is a request for discussion during stage two. The first stage is just for the voicing of issues. These issues will be resolved in the second stage. It is inappropriate for Mom to explain anything or offer an excuse. Her role at this point is to simply acknowledge that the issue exists and perhaps offer an apology to Elaine.

When we explain or offer excuses, we are invalidating the person with whom we are at odds. It's just a way for Mom to justify not showing up on time. The truth of it is, she either should have been there if she gave her word, or, at the very least, called to remake the agreement prior to being late so that Elaine would not feel like Mom is just blowing her off.

During Stage 1, when anyone delivers a Problem, Concern, or Irritation *and wants a Solution to the issue,* he/she should conclude by saying, "I have a Request." The recorder immediately notes the Request. ALL REQUESTS ARE HANDLED IN STAGE 2!

STAGE 2: REQUESTS FOR IDEAS, SOLUTIONS AND PROMISES

Stage 2 of the meeting is organized around Requests to generate Ideas, Solutions and Promises. Begin with the Requests left over from the previous meeting, then move to Requests expressed in Stage 1 of the current meeting, and finally random Requests brought to the meeting by individuals.

Typically during the first few meetings, everyone has issues to sort through, which means plenty of Requests. There are almost always Requests to handle. They may taper off in subsequent meetings. This is a great environment in which most unresolved issues result in a win-win Solution for the family.

During this second stage, the leader/facilitator supports the family members, encourages good listening habits, stops any interruptions and keeps everyone calm and focused on viable Solutions. There are no strict guidelines to follow with Requests. However, when a Request is made, the receiver can negotiate a resolution agreeable to all individuals involved. This process may take some time.

From time to time, the adult coach may have to intercede, to support the leader/facilitator or other members of the family, enforcing the meeting guidelines when necessary.

EXAMPLE OF A FOLLOW-UP TO A
REQUEST FROM A PREVIOUS MEETING

Recorder says, *"John, last week you promised to clean up your room. Did it happen?"*

It did or it didn't. If not, remake the agreement, or negotiate it. After handling requests from the previous meeting, the recorder refers to the list generated in the current meeting.

Next, the leader/facilitator takes back the meeting, and says, starting with the person he/she originally began with, "Do you have any Requests you brought to the meeting?" This process continues until all Requests from all members are expressed.

Agreements during Requests should be resolved in a timely fashion. If they require additional time, it is acceptable to work them out later, thereby maintaining a reasonable time constraint for the meeting.

STAGE 3: THANK YOU'S AND ACKNOWLEDGMENTS

The third and final stage of the meeting is by far the most joyful. This is where the hurts, upsets and disappointments really disappear!

Giving each member of the family Thank you's or Acknowledgments is the most powerful part of the meeting. People are often moved to tears of happiness. Hugs and kisses are welcomed here!

Over time, many families begin to resolve differences on an individual basis, using *The Family Connection* process as a background. Often, subsequent meetings will reveal fewer Problems, Concerns or Irritations, as well as fewer requests, marked by an abundance of warm exchanges. What a wonderful difference that makes! These are the positive signs that family members are indeed connecting – happy evidence that *The Family Connection* is working in your home!

There is no special way to give acknowledgment, but it is a good idea to be as specific as possible. An example is as follows:

Mom might say to her daughter, "Fiona, you have really buckled down and gotten your schedule organized. I am proud to see you completing your homework on time and making time to get your chores done. I know it hasn't been easy to juggle all your activities. But you're doing a fine job and I appreciate your help and hard work." This is so much more effective than a simple, "I'm proud of you; thanks for your help."

ACCEPTING ACKNOWLEDGMENTS AS A GIFT

Some family members may struggle with Acknowledgments, both in giving and receiving them. When someone reminds you of your uniqueness, the mind may ask, "Do I deserve this praise?" The mind usually then answers, "No!" The praise is tuned out as the individual feels it isn't deserved. Looking for a hidden motive, he/she subconsciously asks, "What does the praise-giving individual want?"

Here is the only true answer: An Acknowledgment is simply a gift of grace, love and appreciation from one person to another. The appropriate response is an expression of thanks. This kindness, extended honestly, touches the heart and dissolves the hurts – both real and perceived – and provides family unity and harmony

ENDING THE MEETING COMPLETION OF THE MEETING

When all thank yous and acknowledgments are delivered, the leader/facilitator asks, "Is there anything anyone needs to say before we end this meeting?" Be sure each family member responds to this question and that everyone is left feeling whole, nurtured, and acknowledged.

HOW TO IMPROVE MEETINGS

Write it down! Family meetings proceed much easier, faster and with less stress when everyone comes to them prepared. Preparing in advance frees your mind for listening. For Stages 2 and 3, simply jot down the points you want to discuss, so valuable meeting time won't be spent waiting on each other.

Why listening is important. The average person is a poor listener. This is because we comprehend information four times faster than the rate of speech, therefore have time for extraneous thoughts. These extraneous thoughts interfere significantly with listening. This also is a sign that our attention is on ourselves rather than the other person.

Listening carefully allows everyone to explain what is really important; each family member can direct his/her message precisely to the other person. Listening gives the family member an opportunity to become involved in the discussion, thus increasing the likelihood of a positive conclusion.

Think like the family member. The problems and needs of others are important. You will understand better if you consider the other family member's point of view.

Listen for ideas, not just words. You want to get the whole picture, not just the isolated bits and pieces. The leader/facilitator can clarify by asking, "what do you mean?" The adult coach may assist at any time.

Concentrate. Focus your mind on what the family member is

saying. Practice shutting out distractions.

Don't interrupt. A pause, even a long one, does not mean the person has finished saying everything he/she wishes. Be patient. Hear the other person out.

Use reflective phrases. To elaborate the point, use a reflective phrase, such as, "You said," "you mentioned," "you cited before," "you described." After repeating the statement, follow through with a question beginning with *who, what, when, where,* or *how.*

React to ideas, not to the person. Remember, a family meeting isn't about changing people. It is about listening, being heard and respected, and expressing love and appreciation.

If you hear something someone said that you do not like or appreciate, remember, you promised a safe environment. And you promised to listen. The person is not the problem. By interacting with them as if they were the problem, you invalidate them. This is costly to affinity and harmony. The best way to keep the situation in perspective is to ask questions. For example, Mom may say to Dad, "I don't like how fast you drive." Rather than defending why he drives fast, Dad might diffuse his reaction by saying, "What's fast driving to you? What speed is too fast? What speed would you recommend I drive?" When you ask questions, you clarify the situation and learn the other person's perspective. To some, eighty miles per hour is too fast. To others, sixty is the top limit of fast. When you separate the person from the action and find out that other point of view, you can then compromise and negotiate an acceptable driving speed that works for both parties. You haven't changed the person, you have acknowledged a situation, negotiated it and changed the behavior.

Give up arguing mentally. Don't allow yourself to be irritated at things you hear or the manner they are presented. It will only distract you.

Usually if you are interacting with another person, there are two other conversations going on. You're having one in your head about the other person or what they are saying, and the other person is having one in his head about you. It is reasonably accurate to say that there are three conversations going on, rather than one. If you are engaged in your own mental conversation, you are not listening completely to what the other person is saying. You may or may not agree, but that's not the point. Put yourself in their shoes so you can actually hear what they are trying to tell you from their point of view. When you let go of your mental conversation, you are completely available and can resolve the issue much faster and easier.

Don't jump to conclusions. Avoid making unwarranted assumptions. Do not mentally complete other's sentences.

From time to time all of us have been interrupted while someone attempted to finish our thought in order to hasten the conversation. Often, it's not even close to what you really wanted to say. Be patient. Allow the other person to express his thoughts in his own way and in his own time. Be compassionate and totally available. Let the other person express his view, even if you totally disagree with it. Another way of saying it is, *Be* in relationship with another person rather than *Do* a relationship with another person.

Use listening responses, An occasional "Yes," "I see," or "uh-huh," shows the person you are still with them and compels them to continue.

Listen for overtones. You can learn a great deal about the *way* they state things and how they react to the things you say. Be careful, though. Avoid "*mind reading.*" Ask for clarification until you are *sure* of the real issue.

Practice listening every day. Use conversations with friends, family and fellow students/workers as a tool to improve your listening skills. "Sharpen your inner ear."

KEEPING THE HARMONY GOING

The family meeting process takes time. It is not an instant fix. It takes time, involvement and commitment. The facilitator needs to review the materials here. The coach needs to be well acquainted with the materials also. Family members need to take the time to write down the Problems, Concerns, and Irritations that they are facing.

The family meeting needs time. Schedule your meetings when all family members can attend. I recommend that the family hold meetings weekly for a couple of months. This gives the family and opportunity to learn the process and resolve old conflicts and issues. As you continue with the process, you will see, as the old conflicts are resolved, the family coming together with fewer conflicts, fewer issues to resolve. The meetings then become an occasion for affirmation. The meetings take on an energy, a blessedness that fulfills each of its members. I have found that most people, once they are well acquainted with the process, resolve disputes outside the meeting. With the tools they have acquired, the resolution of conflict becomes easier, less stressful, and the results are much more profound.

Certainly, by then, the need for weekly (or more often) meetings becomes less. Despite the lack of conflict, though, the family meetings are a great way for the family to maintain contact.

CHAPTER 10

Just a Few Final Comments...

Well, there you have it. This book is the end result of twenty years of dialogue with more than fifty thousand people. For interested parties, this work can also be obtained in a video and audiotape format. See page 181.

I used the process for many years in the business world. In fact, that is where it started. I would go to offices and seminars across the country and teach businesses how to communicate through this process. It is possible to use this process everywhere. Even though the people you are in contact with have had no training in the process, if you stick to the principles, you will find yourself able to lead the interaction and accomplish the goal. Others may not even be aware of the steps being taken; all they know is the conflict has been resolved and no one is raging or feeling used and abused.

A parent once told me of a conversation she'd had with her child's teacher: "What are you doing to Jimmy?" She asked. "Excuse me?" the mother replied. "What are you doing to Jimmy? He is the best child in my class. He is no longer disruptive, he is helpful, he completes his work on time."

"He's a pleasure to have in the classroom!" This mother was as amazed as the teacher. She had seen improvement at home, but she never dreamed that the results would carry over to school! It was all the result of having effective "family meetings!"

This type of change, this type of growth is possible at any stage of life. Simply put, if the consequence is age appropriate, the family can take advantage of all the resources that its members contribute. A child's view is often the clearest. The family needs that vision, that clarity. Each child, no matter his or her age, has the ability to help the family resolve conflicts, to create harmony and bring the family closer to each other.

A teacher I know utilized the process in her Montessori class. She assumed the role of facilitator and coach, as the children were very young four, five and six year-olds. I was invited one day to observe the meeting. These children were amazing! There was order, the children did not speak out of turn. They were able to express their concerns, resolve them and acknowledge each other without upset or anger. The teacher later explained to me that she had observed the children in their interactions outside the meeting. She said they often used the process to resolve differences in the classroom and on the playground. The children were more observant and more tolerant than previous classes that had not used the process.

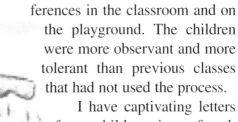

Life is an interpretation – you always have a choice!

I have captivating letters from children in a fourth grade class who were taught the process. In that case, the class had issues with one student in particular. John (not his real name) was whiny, rude, and obnoxious. The class decided in a team meeting that they would work on being nice to John, to "make him great," to see if their attitude toward him could help him change his behavior. So for a few days, the members of the class worked extra hard at making John great. They said hello to him when they crossed paths. They picked him first for the games. They assisted him with assignments and talked to him during recess.

The change in John was no less than miraculous. He quit whining. He quit trying to get attention by disrupting the class. He tried harder on the playground. John was a new person and this new person was one that his classmates and teacher liked. John had more confidence and realized that 'good' attention is so much more fun than 'bad' attention. I would like to share one of these letters with you:

Dear Mr. Elliott:

My classmates and I have been participating in the communication meeting since September. Some ways it has made a difference in our lives is when you tell people in the circle you want them to stop doing things, they have to stop doing what they have been doing. Also, the way you tell them to stop, you're telling it to them in a nice way so they don't get all upset. And sometimes you don't like to talk to your friends that way, but it helps you and your friends. Also, people say nice things about you in the communication circle. They say things like thank you for playing with me at recess and things like that. Some ways it has made a difference in our lives is by making [it] easier to say things without being embarrassed. It also made a difference in John's* life. John used to be considered a nerd, jerk, baby, etc. and I must say, he acted like a nerd, jerk, baby, etc. I think he acted like this because his father died. But then our class became very nice to him. He changed a whole lot. Now other people are nice to him, too. He used to be sort of mean. And whenever he would fall down, he pretends to cry. He doesn't do those kind of things anymore. So I think it's made a difference in his life and I think it's made a difference in our lives, too, because he doesn't push us down or hit us anymore! [When] our class became very nice to John, he changed a lot, we changed a lot and now other people are nice to him too. Now John has lots of friends, and I am one of them!

Your friend, Mary Ann

P.S. It feels great to make a difference in someone's life.
P.S. number 2. Now I can say things to my mother that I could never say before.

* Name has been changed

This incredibly insightful letter is just one of many I have received from children who have learned the communication process. All this due to a small change in perspective.

One time, Dr. Wayne W. Dyer and I were sharing a stage. Near the conclusion of his remarks to the audience, Wayne spoke about what life is really about. Using the child's song, "Row, row, row your boat," he emphasized it by saying, "Row, row, row your boat, *gently* down the stream." As he spoke and the magic of those powerful words set in, almost spontaneously, someone in the room started singing the song. Within seconds, a thousand people came to their feet and sang together, "Row, row, row your boat, gently down the stream…" I stepped off the stage with tears in my eyes, being so moved, while Wayne continued to lead the singing. It was almost as if the audience didn't want to put it down. They had found magic in those simple words and they wanted to remain in the moment.

The real magic for me is in communication. It's not always easy; it's often challenging and frustrating. From time to time, no matter what you do, it doesn't quite turn out. Occasionally, I step back to look at my purpose here. I have gone through many phases, and at this time, my conclusion is that we are all here for a purpose. Some call it karma. Some call it following God's plan. Whatever interpretation we give it, the one thing I am sure of, is that we are all in this together. Life is much easier for each of us when we come from a point of view that speaks about 'you and me.' Often I see the point of view, 'you *or* me,' which leaves someone out. It's not unlike a situation where one group has all the water. They don't share it with everyone in an appropriate way. At some point in time, 'they' (whomever that is) will come and take the water away. I like how Buckminster Fuller said it: "The whole world belongs to everyone." He felt that when a child was born it would be given a number of credits. As it grew older, the child could use those credits for anything. They could use them to buy a house, they could use them to become a coal miner, an airline pilot – it didn't matter; they could use those credits in any manner they chose. After all, not everyone wants to be a pilot, maybe they want to be a coal miner.

If everyone had an equal amount of credits to do what they wished, the world would be a happier place. His point is well taken. The world does belong to all of us. I can recall learning how the Native Americans were surprised and could not understand how the White Man wanted to own land. Their belief was, "How can anyone *own* land? Doesn't it belong to all of the Creator's creatures?"

In my lifetime, I doubt that I will see that world unity. But the world does belong to all of us, and in the land of communication, the land of you and me, the land of peace and harmony, the world is ours, and does belong to all of us.

My intention in writing this book was to share, from my perspective, a small piece of the world that I have been exposed to and been blessed to participate in. People from all walks of life, all over this great land, have opened up their hearts to me along the way and have shared parts of their journey with me. I have had the great opportunity to be contributed to, much more than I have ever been able to give back. I am optimistic that our culture, and indeed the entire world, will ultimately change course from the ground of being of '*you or me*' (which leaves someone out) to '*you and me*' (which includes all). I'd like to share with you one last story; one that says it all:

Two battleships assigned to the training squadron had been at sea on maneuvers in heavy weather for several days. I was serving on the lead battleship and was on watch on the bridge as night fell. The visibility was poor, there was patchy fog. So the captain remained on the bridge, keeping eye on all activities. Shortly after dark, the lookout on the wing of the bridge reported, "Light, bearing on the starboard bow."

The captain then called to the signal man, "Signal that ship; we are on a collision course, advise you change course twenty degrees."

Back came a signal, "It's advisable for you to change course twenty degrees."

The captain said, "Send, I am a captain, change course twenty degrees."

"I'm a seaman second class," came the reply. "You had better change course twenty degrees."

By that time the captain was furious. He spat out, "Send, I'm a battleship. Change course twenty degrees."

Back came the flashing light, "I'm a lighthouse."

We changed course.[5]

Thank you for your commitment to families and relationships!

– Sonny Elliott

Sonny Elliott,
Family Dynamics Expert

ABOUT THE AUTHOR...

Sonny Elliott is a professional speaker, consultant, coach and trainer. He is currently Director of Relationships for a publicly held company.

His contribution to families, classrooms, and organizations has consistently produced outstanding results in the area of improved relationships and productivity.

His boyhood dream of supporting people from all walks of life in having successful relationships continues to be a major focus.

REFERENCES

1   Scarf, Maggie, *Intimate Worlds, Life Inside the Family,* New York, N.Y., Random House, 1995.

2   Weiss, Michael J., *New Report: Don't Slap Me, Silly,* Newsweek, April 20, 1998 Source: Claritas Inc., NFO Research, Inc.

3   Hesse, Hermann *A Dream Sequence* from *The Fairy Tales of Hermann Hesse*, translated by Jack Zipes, New York, N.Y. Bantam Books, 1995.

4   Chapin, Harry, *Cat's in the Cradle,* 1987 Cherry Lane Music Co., Inc.

5   Kock, Frank, *Proceedings, The Magazine of the Naval Institute,*

Appendix

QUESTIONS AND ANSWERS

Q. Should one person always be the leader/facilitator?

A. It is best to have the same person be the leader/facilitator for a few months. As the family participates, it will become apparent that *The Family Connection* meeting is actually a learning process. The participants are being shown how to separate or distinguish between being accused and listening to others' realities. As a result, they can take criticism less personally and are empowered to respect the viewpoints of others. Thus, the more you participate in the meeting, the more proficient you become. The leader/facilitator is also engaged in a learning process, developing proficiency and building trust.

Q. What's the best way to teach another leader/facilitator?

A. Before the present leader/facilitator turns his/her job over to another family member, there should be a two- to three-meeting training period. During this time, the new leader/facilitator reads **The Family Connection** process and, perhaps has an adult explain it. Then the trainee would lead/facilitate the next two meetings with the current leader/facilitator acting as coach. After these meetings, the current leader/facilitator and the trainee would have a debriefing session. The trainee can report what worked and what didn't, asking for additional coaching from the adults.

Q. Can we modify or change the process?

A. I have been asked this question often, and in each case, there seems to be a common denominator: The families feel uncomfortable delivering Problems, Concerns, or Irritations in the meeting. Most of the people wanting to change the format want to handle things in private.

When people want to "handle it in private," their attention may be focused on making sure they "look good" rather than finding what works for the family. I am not averse to people addressing their Problems, Concerns, or Irritations right away, without the advantage of a meeting. However, this private handling of issues can only be done effectively when the people involved are fully grounded in the principles of effective communication. Only then can they interact with each other from the point of view of what isn't working, rather than who is right or wrong, and have it turn out positive.

Having said that, I want to make the point about junior and senior conversations. There are things that should not be said in front of the children. These are senior conversations. There are issues that simply should not be handled in front of the children. Sex issues probably should not be handled in front of six and seven year-olds. For instance, your thirteen year-old may have inadvertently stepped in on your lovemaking, creating issues regarding sex and privacy. If you have younger children in the household, then this issue might be best handled in private with just the parents and the thirteen year-old. Of course, the thirteen-year -old may have said something to the younger siblings, thus making it an issue for the entire family. Then it would be appropriate for the family meeting. The bottom line is, this is the parents' judgement call. There is a difference. Senior conversations are for the more mature members of the family, junior conversations are subjects for the entire family.

Q. What should **not** be handled in the meeting?

A. There is almost nothing that cannot be resolved in this process. You must use your own judgement, i.e., adults talking about very personal issues in front of children. You will know instinctively if the subject is or isn't appropriate for the age or temperament of your child.

Q. Can I really express anything in this meeting? What if I'm very angry?

A. Verbally expressing any feeling within the process format (who, when, where, what happened and I felt...) is productive. PHYSICAL EXPRES-

SION OF ANGER IS NEVER PRODUCTIVE. IT IS ALSO NEVER ACCEPTABLE. *The Family Connection* process diffuses extreme anger and allows a Problem, Concern, Irritation to be resolved in a positive and safe manner. If a person is extremely angry and refuses to honor the guidelines of the meeting, then it's highly suggested that the meeting be postponed. People can have meetings when they are upset or when feelings are hurt, but if a person is in a rage, this meeting process is not the answer. It is not designed for that. It is designed to prevent that. If rage is the problem, it would probably be best to seek professional intervention with a qualified therapist.

Q. What if one member of the family will not participate?

A. If the person is a child, insist that they sit in, be part of the family and listen. Usually, once the child sees that it really is safe to communicate feelings and that there are no consequences for expressing themselves, they will be eager, or at least willing to join in.

A reluctant parent will usually be willing to at least be an observer when the family members ask. If not, continue meeting without the parent and continue inviting him/her to participate. Remember, when a person is not at the meeting they are not talked about. Work *only* with those present.

Q. What can we do to get our child to communicate his Problems, Concerns, or Irritations? He always says he doesn't have any.

A. First, the child must be reassured there will be no consequence for speaking his feelings. It sounds good, but how many times has someone told you, "You can trust me," then you found out you couldn't. As the child observes others communicating he will feel safe.

Something that I have never seen fail to get a response is to ask the child, "If you did have a Problem, Concern, or Irritation, what would it be," or, "If you had to pretend you have a problem, what would it be about?"

Q. Would it be enough to do the family meeting for a couple of months until we felt better, then stop?

A. Probably after two months some major Problems, Concerns, or Irritations have been resolved or much improved. The real beauty of this process is in its ongoing use. Families deepen the bonds, trust, respect and admiration for others and themselves. The problems are fewer and the acknowledgments more abundant and profound. The biggest gift we can give each other is our attention and interest. This is a habit worth keeping. When the communication meeting is stopped, there is a tendency to revert back to the old ways of repressed feelings and explosive emotions.

Q. No matter what we do there is a recurring problem about our son not doing his homework and making unsatisfactory grades. How can this be addressed in the family meeting?

A. When you communicate to your son you have a concern about his continued low grades, you ask that he does his homework. If that Request is denied or ignored, then it is time to negotiate – rewards for homework done or consequences for not doing the homework. If he continues to deny or ignore the concern, maybe it is time to give up trying to effect a change. Remember my story of our son, Andy. Let go of the responsibility. Let the child take it. It might be wise to speak with his teacher to let him know what the family has decided to try. Your child's teacher is a great resource. Keep contact and communication open here. Sometimes all we can do is stand by and watch our children, make sure that their road is as safe as possible, that we have instilled a love of mankind and a sense of self, and wish them well. And of course, prayer never hurts.

Remember how we talked earlier about feeding your love and support through simple presence, how you sat near your loved one and sent loving 'vibes' their way. Focus on the love you feel for your child, not on the upsets of their deficiencies at school. Give your love, give your support, unconditionally. As long as there is love, there is room for growth. Sometimes it just takes a little longer.

VOCABULARY FOR EFFECTIVE FAMILY MEETINGS

Guidelines for Sender: Deliver specific communications to individual, without opinions or judgements. Message should be brief and understandable.

Guidelines for Receiver: Acknowledge feelings with nothing added. Do not debate. No zingers. No stories.

EXAMPLES OF FEELINGS ABOUT PROBLEMS, CONCERNS OR IRRITATIONS:

Abandoned	Depressed	Hopeless	Overwhelmed
Angry	Desperate	Humiliated	Perplexed
Annoyed	Devastated	Hurt	Put down
Anxious	Disbelieving	Ignored	Pressured
Bored	Discounted	Insulted	Rejected
Cheated	Disgusted	Irritated	Sickened
Concerned	Distrustful	Judged	Suspicious
Confused	Dominated	Let down	Tense
Controlled	Embarrassed	Low	Tormented
Critical	Frightened	Manipulated	Trampled
Criticized	Frustrated	Misunderstood	Unheard
Cut off	Hateful	Nauseated	Uptight
Deceived	Harried	Offended	Used

EXAMPLES OF ACKNOWLEDGEMENTS

Accepted	Elated	Interested	Safe
Admired	Energized	Invigorated	Satisfied
Affirmed	Exalted	Liberated	Soft
Amused	Excited	Loved	Stimulated
Appreciated	Exhilarated	Mellow	Strong
Calm	Friendly	Optimistic	Supported
Cared for	Fulfilled	Passionate	Thrilled
Caring	Gentle	Playful	Understood
Cheered	Grateful	Real	Valued
Cheerful	Gratified	Reassured	Vindicated
Confident	Happy	Recognized	Wanted
Comfortable	Heard	Refreshed	Warm
Delighted	Honored	Relaxed	Worthy
Encouraged	Hopeful	Relieved	
Ecstatic	Inspired	Respected	

COMMUNICATION WORKSHEET

TO WHOM:_____

WHEN: _____WHERE: _____

WHAT ACTUALLY HAPPENED OR WHAT WAS ACTUALLY SAID:

_____

_____

"I FELT _____"

COMMUNICATION WORKSHEET

TO WHOM:_____

WHEN: _____WHERE: _____

WHAT ACTUALLY HAPPENED OR WHAT WAS ACTUALLY SAID:

_____

_____

"I FELT _____"

COMMUNICATION WORKSHEET

TO WHOM:_____

WHEN: _____WHERE: _____

WHAT ACTUALLY HAPPENED OR WHAT WAS ACTUALLY SAID:

_____

_____

"I FELT _____"

COMMUNICATION WORKSHEET

TO WHOM:_____

WHEN: _____WHERE: _____

WHAT ACTUALLY HAPPENED OR WHAT WAS ACTUALLY SAID:

_____

_____

"I FELT _____"

COMMUNICATION WORKSHEET

TO WHOM:_____

WHEN: _____WHERE: _____

WHAT ACTUALLY HAPPENED OR WHAT WAS ACTUALLY SAID:

_____

_____

"I FELT _____"

COMMUNICATION WORKSHEET

TO WHOM:_____

WHEN: _____WHERE: _____

WHAT ACTUALLY HAPPENED OR WHAT WAS ACTUALLY SAID:

_____

_____

"I FELT _____"

COMMUNICATION WORKSHEET

TO WHOM:_____

WHEN: _____WHERE: _____

WHAT ACTUALLY HAPPENED OR WHAT WAS ACTUALLY SAID:

_____

_____

"I FELT _____"

COMMUNICATION WORKSHEET

TO WHOM:_____

WHEN: _____WHERE: _____

WHAT ACTUALLY HAPPENED OR WHAT WAS ACTUALLY SAID:

_____

_____

"I FELT _____"

THANK YOU, APPRECIATION, AND ACKNOWLEDGEMENT FORM

I, _____ would like to thank you for

_____

_____

_____

_____

_____

THANK YOU, APPRECIATION, AND ACKNOWLEDGEMENT FORM

I, _____ would like to thank you for

_____

_____

_____

_____

_____

THANK YOU, APPRECIATION, AND ACKNOWLEDGEMENT FORM

I, _____ would like to thank you for

_____

_____

_____

_____

_____

THANK YOU, APPRECIATION, AND ACKNOWLEDGEMENT FORM

I, _____ would like to thank you for

_____

_____

_____

_____

_____

THANK YOU, APPRECIATION, AND ACKNOWLEDGEMENT FORM

I, _____ would like to thank you for

_____

_____

_____

_____

_____

THANK YOU, APPRECIATION, AND ACKNOWLEDGEMENT FORM

I, _____ would like to thank you for

_____

_____

_____

_____

_____

THANK YOU, APPRECIATION, AND ACKNOWLEDGEMENT FORM

I, _____ would like to thank you for

_____

_____

_____

_____

_____

THANK YOU, APPRECIATION, AND ACKNOWLEDGEMENT FORM

I, _____ would like to thank you for

_____

_____

_____

_____

_____

REQUEST FORM

I REQUEST _____
_____
_____
_____
_____
_____
_____

REQUEST FORM

I REQUEST _____
_____
_____
_____
_____
_____
_____

REQUEST FORM

I REQUEST _____
_____
_____
_____
_____
_____
_____

REQUEST FORM

I REQUEST _____
_____
_____
_____
_____
_____
_____

REQUEST FORM

I REQUEST _____

_____

_____

_____

_____

_____

_____

REQUEST FORM

I REQUEST _____

_____

_____

_____

_____

_____

_____

REQUEST FORM

I REQUEST _____

_____

_____

_____

_____

_____

_____

REQUEST FORM

I REQUEST _____

_____

_____

_____

_____

_____

_____

SONNY ELLIOTT AND THE FAMILY CONNECTION SERIES
AS ADVERTISED ON NATIONAL TV!

Thank you for your purchase. I am proud to offer this communication process to you and I trust that when you follow the process, you will find your relationships more fun, less stressful, and infinitely more productive.

In addition to this book, the Family Connection Series offers three, separate audio-visual programs:

The Family Connection shows how families can work together in a family meeting to communicate Problems, Concerns, and Irritations in a safe, honest and accepting environment. The meeting process is simple, so simple, in fact, that an eight year-old can (and should) facilitate meetings. In this process, the family can solve problems, find compromise, and give each other the support and acknowledgment that strengthens family ties.

The Couple Connection helps to rekindle the spark of passion. Through this process, couples make time for each other, communicate freely, and strengthen their love in an intimate and trusting climate. It breaks down the barriers and helps to enforce the foundation of a true and lasting love. The Couple Connection helps lovers to focus and gives them the road map to a successful relationship.

The Teen Connection gives families the resources to help their adolescents through probably the most terrifying and exciting time in their lives. Through the Town Hall Meeting, teens can voice their issues without fear of retribution and with confidence and clarity. The Teen Connection can bring the issues of school, sex, drugs, violence, and peer pressure into a milieu where they can be dealt with and resolved. Parents can, through The Teen Connection, help their offspring make the transition to adulthood a great deal smoother, all the while saving their own sanity. The Teen Connection is essential in these turbulent times.

*We are proud to be presenting these worthwhile programs in a complete, easy to follow process. With three videos, four audio's, and guidebook, the **Family, Couple,** and **Teen Connection** programs are fun to watch, hear, and read. Show the ones you love just how much you care. Open the door to an improved life for you and your family. Order your program today!*

Each program is only $89.99 + S&H!

SEND A COPY OF THIS BOOK TO SOMEONE YOU LOVE!

"Mom, Dad Are You Listening" is an ideal book for families, classes, and groups. Get quantity discounts when you order multiple copies for your loved ones, friends, or students.

3-199 copies	= $9.83 per book + S&H
200-499 copies	= $8.75 per book + S&H
500+ copies	= $7.65 per book + S&H

To order, and for shipping information, please contact BOOKMASTERS at:
e-mail: order@bookmaster.com
or
800-247-6553
FAX: 419-281-6883
or
BOOKMASTERS INC.
P.O. Box 388
Ashland, OH 44805
Web site: http://www.bookmaster.com

ALSO AVAILABLE

Sonny Elliott Live: This audio series (two tapes, 90 minutes each) discusses communication in all facets of our lives. From work, to home, to our daily contact with others, these audio's help us communicate more effectively. They are available separately, or as a set.

Focusing, Languaging, and Boundaries ....$18.95 + S&H
Belief Systems, Rules, and Survival Strategies ....$18.95 + S&H
Coaching Principles for Conflict Resolution ....$18.95 + S&H
Context for Family Meetings ....$18.95 + S&H

The Stress Connection This 90-minute audiotape
discusses the sources of stress in our daily lives and
gives guidelines for reducing that stress. ....$9.95 + S&H

Note:
I am available for group presentations, personal telephone coaching, and in-house consulting.

I can be contacted through SKYSTONE PUBLICATIONS at:
P.O. Box 18731, Reno, NV. 89511-9269
OR: e-mail: sonny@sonnyelliott.com

Mom, Dad, Are You Listening?

ORDER FORM

DESCRIPTION	UNIT PRICE	QTY.	TOTAL
1) **The Family Connection** Two 90-minute videotapes; One 90-minute coaching video Four audio-tapes; Guidebook	$89.99	____	____
The Couple Connection Two videotapes: 60-min. & 35-min.; One 2-hour coaching video Four audio-tapes; Guidebook	$89.99	____	____
The Teen Connection Two 75-minute videotapes; One 90-minute coaching video Four audio-tapes; Guidebook *Shipping & Handling per order*	$89.99 $12.95	____	____
2) **Focusing, Languaging, and Boundaries**	$18.95	____	____
Coaching Principles for Conflict Resolution	$18.95	____	____
***Belief Systems, Rules and Survival Strategies**	$18.95	____	____
***Context for Family Meetings**	$18.95	____	____
Shipping & Handling per order	$ 6.95	____	____
3) **Any Two Audio Programs**	$29.95	____	____
4) **All Four Audio Programs**	$49.95	____	____
5) **The Stress Connection**	$9.95	____	____
Shipping & Handling	$ 2.95	____	____

Special Offer: *Order any "Connection" Video program, Audio Program, and "The Stress Connection," and save on shipping and handling* $14.95 ____

Subtotal ____

* **Included in The Family Connection Video Album**

TOTAL ____

Please Print

Name _____

Address _____

City_____ State _____ Zip_____ Phone _____

❏ MasterCard ❏ Visa ❏ American Express

#_____ Exp. _____ Signature _____

Please enclose payment, check or money order and mail to or call:

800-247-6553 • FAX: 419-281-6883
or
BOOKMASTERS INC.
P.O. Box 388
Ashland, OH 44805
Web site: http://www.bookmaster.com